BOMBERS
OF WORLD WARS I AND II

BOMBERS
OF WORLD WARS I AND II

FRANCIS CROSBY

southwater

For Gemma.
Special thanks are due to Derek and
Marjorie Brammer for their considerable help
with research and administration.

This edition is published by Southwater

Southwater is an imprint of Anness Publishing Ltd
Hermes House, 88–89 Blackfriars Road, London SE1 8HA
tel. 020 7401 2077; fax 020 7633 9499
www.southwaterbooks.com; info@anness.com

UK agent: The Manning Partnership Ltd, 6 The Old Dairy,
Melcombe Road, Bath BA2 3LR; tel. 01225 478444;
fax 01225 478440; sales@manning-partnership.co.uk

UK distributor: Grantham Book Services Ltd, Isaac Newton Way,
Alma Park Industrial Estate, Grantham, Lincs NG31 9SD;
tel. 01476 541080; fax 01476 541061; orders@gbs.tbs-ltd.co.uk

North American agent/distributor: National Book Network,
4501 Forbes Boulevard, Suite 200, Lanham, MD 20706;
tel. 301 459 3366; fax 301 429 5746; www.nbnbooks.com

Australian agent/distributor: Pan Macmillan Australia,
Level 18, St Martins Tower,
31 Market St,
Sydney, NSW 2000;
tel. 1300 135 113; fax 1300 135 103;
customer.service@macmillan.com.au

New Zealand agent/distributor: David Bateman Ltd,
30 Tarndale Grove, Off Bush Road,
Albany, Auckland;
tel. (09) 415 7664; fax (09) 415 8892

Publisher: Joanna Lorenz
Editorial Director: Judith Simons
Project Editor: Felicity Forster
Copy Editors: Judy Cox and Jeremy Nichols
Designer: Ian Sandom
Production Controller: Claire Rae

Previously published as part of a larger volume, *Bombers*

1 3 5 7 9 10 8 6 4 2

PAGE 1: **Boeing B-17 Flying Fortress.** PAGES 2–3: **Grumman Avenger.** BELOW: **Avro Lancaster.**

Contents

6 Introduction

The History of World War Bombers

10 Birth of the bomber

12 Early bombing raids

14 Bomber aircraft technology up to 1945

16 Bombers of the Spanish Civil War

18 The Blitz

20 The Dambusters

22 The Mighty Eighth Air Force

24 The Doolittle raid

26 The atomic bomb raids

A–Z of World War Bombers: 1914–45

30 Aichi D3A

30 Amiot 143

31 Arado Ar 234 Blitz

32 Armstrong Whitworth Whitley

34 Avro Anson

35 Avro Manchester

36 Avro Lancaster

38 Boeing B-17 Flying Fortress

40 Boeing B-29 Superfortress

42 Breguet Bre.14

42 Breguet Bre.19

43 Breguet 691/693

44 Bristol Blenheim

46 Bristol Beaufighter

48 Consolidated B-24 Liberator

50 Consolidated PBY-5A Catalina

52 Curtiss SB2C Helldiver

53 de Havilland/Airco DH4

53 de Havilland/Airco DH9A

54 de Havilland/Airco DH10 Amiens

56 de Havilland Mosquito

58 Dornier Do17

59 Dornier Do217

60 Douglas B-18 Bolo

61 Douglas SBD-5 Dauntless

62 Douglas A-20 Boston/ Havoc

64 Douglas A-26/B-26 Invader

66 Fairey Swordfish

68 Fairey Battle

70 Fairey Barracuda

72 Focke-Wulf Fw200

74 Gotha bombers

76 Grumman Avenger

78 Handley Page Halifax

80 Handley Page Hampden

81 Handley Page Heyford

82 Handley Page O/400

83 Hawker Typhoon

84 Heinkel He111

86 Heinkel He177

88 Ilyushin Il-2 Shturmovik

90 Ilyushin Il-4

92 Junkers Ju 52/3m

94 Junkers Ju 87 Stuka

96 Junkers Ju 88

98 Kawanishi H8K

100 Lockheed Hudson

102 Martin bomber series

103 Martin Maryland

103 Martin Baltimore

104 Martin Mariner

106 Martin B-26 Marauder

108 Mitsubishi G4M

110 North American B-25 Mitchell

112 Short Stirling

114 Short Sunderland

116 Tupolev SB

117 Tupolev TB-3

117 Tupolev Tu-2

118 Vickers Vimy

120 Vickers Virginia

121 Vickers Wellesley

122 Vickers Wellington

124 Vultee Vengeance

125 Yokosuka D4Y Suisei

125 Yokosuka P1Y1

126 Glossary

127 Index

128 Acknowledgements

Introduction

The earliest days of using aircraft as bombers saw pilots tossing small improvised bombs over the side of their aircraft on to rather surprised enemy below. Hitting the target was more luck than judgement. This is a far cry indeed from the bomber aircraft of today that can fly around the world at several hundred miles an hour and arrive undetected in enemy airspace to drop precision-guided bombs down a chimney of a target and destroy it with no damage to surrounding buildings.

Once it was appreciated that the combination of aircraft and bombs was more than a novelty, military strategists were soon calling for more and bigger bombs to be carried. This soon required larger aircraft with more than one engine to carry the greater payload. Range then became an issue as the bombers had to be able to reach targets far beyond the front line.

In addition to a greater understanding of aerodynamics, engine technology and performance became considerations because the bombers had to be able to climb to heights away from enemy guns and fighters or have sufficient speed to outrun the latter. Once the enemy started to try to knock the new bombers out of the sky, then they had to defend themselves by carrying machine-guns and cannon. Technological advances saw the monoplane emerge, then largely replace the biplane in bomber fleets by World War II.

TOP: **The crew of an RAF Coastal Command B-17 Flying Fortress being briefed in 1943.** ABOVE: **Smoke pours from the remains of a bridge in France destroyed by Allied bombers around D-Day, 1944.**

Advances in construction techniques brought the use of more metal, specifically lightweight but strong alloys, and less wood and canvas.

The development of the jet engine during World War II opened up many opportunities for aircraft designers, but the new form of propulsion did not reach its full potential until some years later. Indeed, many long-range piston-engine bombers designed for use in World War II remained in use long after the end of that conflict. Very long-range bombers like the Boeing B-29 Superfortress were developed to attack enemies over great distances. Some consider Germany's lack of long-range heavy bombers to have been a significant factor in their losing the war.

The weaponry available to bomber aircraft reached new levels of destructive capacity in 1945 with the development of atomic bombs. Fleets of bomber aircraft no longer had to carry many thousands of bombs at a time when one massively destructive bomb carried by a single aircraft would do the same job, bringing an enemy to their knees. The two atomic bombs dropped on Japan in 1945 clearly demonstrated in the pre-intercontinental ballistic missile age that the bomber could win a war with just one mission.

However, even an aircraft carrying an atomic bomb was still vulnerable to ground and fighter defences, and could be detected on enemy radar. In the course of World War II, complementary technology produced defensive aids like Window, bundles of thousands of aluminium foil strips, which created a mass of reflections on German radar screens as they fluttered down, making it difficult to distinguish the individual bombers. By the end of the war, however, night-fighters were routinely equipped with radar that could home in on individual bombers in darkness, where once they would have been safe.

The performance figures quoted for each type of bomber in this book should be seen as a broad indicator of an aircraft's capabilities. Aircraft performance and capability can vary considerably even within the same marks of an aircraft type. For example, if bombs are carried, maximum speed can be reduced. Also, the maximum speeds quoted are top speeds achieved at the optimum altitude for that particular aircraft type, and should not be seen as the definitive top speed for an aircraft at all altitudes.

ABOVE: **The ruins of Hiroshima in 1945 bear testimony to the massive destructive power of a single atomic bomb.**

ABOVE: **The Boeing B-29 Superfortress was the most advanced bomber produced during World War II, having a range of over 8045km/5000 miles.**

NOT USED IN EUROPE

Key to flags

For the specification boxes, the national flag that was current at the time of the aircraft's use is shown.

Britain

France

Germany: World War I

Germany: World War II

Italy

Japan

USA

USSR

The History of World War Bombers

From the early improvised bombers of World War I to the atomic bombers that ended World War II, bombers evolved to become a potent weapon at military leaders' disposal. Although the early bombers of World War I were small, unimpressive machines, within a year aircraft designers were producing bombers like the Handley Page 0/400 with a wingspan of 30.48m/100ft, almost as big as the famed Lancaster of World War II.

Developments in engine and airframe technology meant that World War II bombers could carry bomb loads five or six times further and many times heavier than their World War I predecessors. As fighter technology developed, so did the defensive armament of the bombers, perhaps typified by the aptly named Boeing B-17 Flying Fortress that bristled with up to 14 guns. The ultimate bomber development within the period covered in this book was the B-17 successor in USAAF service, the B-29 Superfortress. With a range of 5229km/3250 miles and the ability to reach altitudes of 9695m/ 31,800ft, the ultimate World War II bomber was chosen for the ultimate mission – the first atomic bomb raid.

LEFT: **North American B-25 Mitchell.**

The Russian plane Ilya Mourometz, designed by Igor Sikorsky, was the
world's first four-engined aircraft, and could fly over great distances for
the time. ABOVE: **An Italian-operated example of the pioneering Voisin bomber.**
This version was powered by a 190hp Isotta-Franschini V.4B engine.

Birth of the bomber

Although the US Army was the first to drop a bomb from an aeroplane in 1910, it was the Italians who first dropped them in anger against the Turks in 1911. Few of the early bombs were purpose-made, and modified artillery shells fitted with fins were common, sometimes tossed over the side of the aircraft or suspended alongside or beneath the aircraft and dropped at the right time (again trial and error played a large part in this) by the removal of a pin or even a piece of string. While nations debated the morals of bombing and the most effective technique, the Italians simply got on with learning the hard way – at war. It is worth considering that aircraft were operating as bombers some years before the evolution of the scouts that became fighters.

> "Another popular fallacy is to suppose that flying machines could be used to drop dynamite on an enemy in time of war."
> William H. Pickering,
> *Aeronautics*, 1908

Before the start of World War I, the Austro-Hungarians, French, Germans and Russians were all developing specialized bomber aircraft to carry ordnance to and then drop it on a target. Britain had experimented with dropping bombs from aircraft pre-war, but did not build dedicated bombing aircraft until after war had broken out. Many different types of aircraft were used for bombing early in the war, some having the ability to carry an observer or bombs in place of the observer. However, the key to making bombing a potential war-winning military tool was to develop an aircraft that could defend itself while carrying a large cargo of bombs to the heart of the enemy's location.

The first true bomber aircraft used in combat was the French-designed Voisin. Of steel frame construction, the Voisin had a crew of two plus up to 60kg/132lb of bombs. Power was provided by a 70hp engine that drove a pusher propeller. The Voisin earned its spurs when attacking Zeppelin hangars at Metz-Frascaty on August 14, 1914. The pioneering aircraft remained in production throughout World War I and was improved constantly, with engine power increasing from 70hp to 155hp. Most impressive was the increase in bomb load up to 300kg/ 660lb by the end of hostilities.

The French Aviation Militaire began to organize its Voisins into bomber squadrons in September 1914, and eventually had a bomber force of over 600 aircraft which conducted a sustained bombing campaign on the Western Front from May 1915.

On the Eastern Front, the Imperial Russian Air Service soon followed the French lead, and were equipped with the world's first four-engine aircraft, the Ilya Mourometz, designed by Igor Sikorsky. This large aircraft, very advanced for the time, had its first flight in May 1913 and was developed to carry up to 999kg/2200lb of bombs. The most advanced version could remain airborne for five hours at altitudes of around 2743m/9000ft at speeds of 85mph. The type carried out the first of over 400 bombing missions on the Eastern Front in February 1915.

The nations that fought in World War I all had differing views on bombing strategies. Britain's Royal Naval Air Service, Royal Flying Corps and then the Royal Air Force focused on the tactical use of bombing in support of ground troops – the British would also carry out revenge attacks if they felt that the enemy had overstepped the mark.

French planners did not have aircraft in their inventory that would reach Germany, and were in the difficult position of not wanting to bomb areas of France occupied by Germany. In addition, they feared revenge bombing of unoccupied French towns within reach of German aircraft. Meanwhile, Germany was developing aircraft that could cross France and strike at London itself.

TOP: **A classic photograph of a World War II RAF bomber over its target during a bombing raid.** ABOVE: **A detailed photograph of a German Gotha bomber's bomb load.** BELOW LEFT: **British Avro 504s of the Royal Naval Air Service made an early bombing raid on the Zeppelin factory at Freidrichshafen in November 1914.** BELOW: **An early propaganda photograph showing a manual bomber delivering a personalized bomb by hand.**

Early bombing raids

While the Allies were focusing mainly on military targets for bombing, Germany embraced the concept of the bomber as a psychological weapon to be used against civilians. The experience of the panic caused by early Zeppelin raids over cities spurred the Germans to plan raids against enemy population centres. As early as August 1914 German aircraft were flying over Paris dropping grenades and an invitation to the Paris garrison to surrender. Within six weeks, German Etrich Taube aircraft had dropped 56 bombs, none of them heavier than 4.5kg/10lb, which killed 11 Parisians and injured a further 47.

The Germans' tactical use of bombers in World War I is well illustrated by the 1917 German attack on a British supply train prior to the Battle of Mesines Ridge. As a result of the disruption to their supply of ammunition, British artillery had to cease firing after three hours.

Britain's early bombing successes began with Royal Naval Air Service raids on the Zeppelin sheds at Düsseldorf and Cologne on October 8, 1914. The aircraft used were two Sopwith Tabloids. The plane attacking Cologne failed to find its target due to bad weather and bombed the railway station instead, but the other Tabloid successfully dropped a small number of 9kg/20lb bombs on the airship shed, destroying it and Zeppelin Z.9 in the process. The sheds had been targeted before by B.E.2s on September 22, but bad weather and unexploding bombs meant that the mission failed.

Britain was keen to build a dedicated bomber force, and in December 1914 the Admiralty called for the development of a large hard-hitting bomber described by Commodore Murray F. Sueter as a "bloody paralyser of an aeroplane". The resulting Handley Page O/100 entered service with the Royal Naval Air

LEFT: **A selection of German bombs used during World War I. Size of munitions grew as larger aircraft became available.** BELOW: **The Etrich Taube carried out early raids over Paris in August 1914 during World War I. At the start of the war, Taubes were operated by wealthy individuals as well as by the Imperial German forces.**

Service in November 1916, and was used at first for daylight sea patrols near Flanders. From March the following year, the O/100s focused on night-bombing of German naval bases, railway stations and junctions, and industrial targets.

Attacks against weapon-manufacturing facilities were an effective means of removing a threat at source. In 1915 Allied aircraft set out to attack a factory at Ludwigshafen suspected of manufacturing chlorine gas dropped on Allied troops.

A long-range bomber had always been a German priority so that the British mainland would be within reach. In autumn 1916 the Gotha G.V appeared, and this very capable aircraft gave Germany the ability to strike at Britain itself.

On May 25, 1917, a fleet of 21 Gothas attacked the English coastal town of Folkestone, killing 95 inhabitants. The raid caused widespread panic among a populace who now believed that Germany could rain death from the sky over Britain unopposed. At midday on June 13 another fleet of Gothas dropped bombs on London, and the daily raids continued for a month, largely unopposed by the RNAS and Royal Flying Corps. The effect on civilian morale was considerable and damaging, and workers' productivity levels plummeted. The psychological impact was perhaps as damaging to Britain as the loss of life and physical destruction caused by the falling bombs.

The arrival into service of the Sopwith Camel forced the Gothas to switch to night-bombing, which caused the cost to the Germans to climb. Bombing accuracy fell, accidents happened in night-flying and aircraft were shot down for little gain, so the raids ceased before the end of the war. The raids had been damaging for Britain: 835 civilians were killed, 2000 were wounded and there had been three million pounds worth of damage (an enormous amount of money in 1918). However, the morale and productivity problems among the population were even more damaging, and showed the world that the bomber could be a war-winner.

TOP: **A Gotha G.V bomber. These aircraft spread terror among civilians in southern England following raids on the coast and over London in 1917. Daily daylight raids on the capital began in June 1917, launched from bases in Belgium.**
ABOVE: **Soldiers amidst the remains of a house destroyed by a Zeppelin raid over Kings Lynn in Norfolk, England, in 1915.**
LEFT: **The figures with this upturned Handley Page O/400 give a clear indication of the aircraft's size. Note the bomb-bay cells exposed between the legs of the fixed undercarriage.**

Bomber aircraft technology up to 1945

"When my brother and I built the first man-carrying flying machine we thought that we were introducing into the world an invention which would make further wars practically impossible." So said one of the fathers of powered flight, Orville Wright, in 1917. When the Wright brothers built their pioneering Wright Flyer in 1903 they used wood as the main material for the wings and fuselage, braced by piano wire for added strength. By the end of World War II, just over four decades later, most bombers were all-metal and had ranges and top speeds that the Wrights could only have dreamt of. The Wright Flyer was a biplane, having two pairs of wings, and also a pusher aircraft, that is, the propeller was used to push the aircraft from behind rather than pull it from the front as in later so-called tractor aircraft.

The pusher arrangement was retained for some early bombers such as the German Gothas, but having the back end of a large aero engine facing into the wind did little for the aerodynamics of pushers, so the tractor configuration finally became the standard in fighters, bombers and other aircraft.

As engine technology improved and speeds increased, drag became a serious design consideration on early aircraft, and aircraft frames were increasingly covered and enclosed with taut fabric to achieve streamlining. This technique was used into the mid-1930s, but by the time of World War II most new bomber aircraft were of all-metal "monocoque" construction. Whilst the early canvas-covered bombers got their structural strength from taut metal bracing wires, the metal skin of the monocoque fuselage (and in time the wings and tail), welded or riveted to a light metal interior framework, provided an incredibly strong construction. The downside of this construction was the damage that would be caused by cannon shells hitting

ABOVE: **The Consolidated B-24 Liberator first flew in December 1939, and was produced in greater numbers than any other bomber in history.** LEFT: **The Junkers Ju 52, a famed airliner, equipped the embryonic and clandestine Luftwaffe formed in the 1930s. It made its bomber debut in 1936 during the Spanish Civil War. By the end of that conflict, the type had dropped 6096 tonnes/ 6000 tons of bombs on Republican targets.**

LEFT: **A Bristol Blenheim production line at Filton, 1938. The high-speed Blenheim could outrun most contemporary fighters when it entered RAF service in 1937. The original aircraft from which the Blenheim derived, the Type 142, was the first British stressed-skin monoplane.** BELOW: **This fascinating reference photograph shows the variety of bombs at RAF Bomber Command's disposal by the end of World War II, ranging from small general-purpose bombs to the large "earthquake" bombs used against specialist targets.**

the metal structure – in canvas-covered aircraft the shells could have passed right through the aircraft, causing little damage.

The Wrights chose a biplane configuration for their Flyer, and this form was used in most early bombers because two pairs of wings generated more lift than one. Pre-World War I accidents had led Britain's government to ban the Royal Flying Corps from using the apparently unstable and unsafe monoplane, and it was not until 1936 that the RAF deployed a monoplane bomber – the Avro Anson. The "Annie" incorporated both old and new aircraft construction techniques – it was a monoplane but its fuselage had a metal framework with a fabric covering. It is worth pointing out that the Soviet Tupolev TB-3 four-engined monoplane was in production from 1929.

Engine technology developed at almost breakneck speed in the time between World Wars I and II. The 1916 DH4 had a top speed of 230kph/143mph and was powered by a 250hp Eagle VIII in-line piston engine. Within a quarter of a century the Wright Double Cyclone (as used in the Grumman Avenger and B-25 Mitchell) was producing 1700hp and the B-29 that carried out the atomic bomb raids had four 2200hp Wright Duplex Cyclone engines.

At the end of World War I, air-cooled radials and in-line piston engines were the dominant engine types, and both had much to commend them. They were developed to the maximum until the jet engine ultimately replaced them both. Germany's Arado Ar 234 pioneered jet bombers in action and carried out raids over Britain in 1944. The Ar 234 was impossible to catch, and more powerful and efficient engines, coupled with improved aerodynamics, enabled bombers to fly higher and faster.

LEFT: **The cockpit of an Avro Lancaster, the most famous of all British bomber aircraft. The "Lanc" was derived from the earlier twin-engine Manchester, and went on to become key to the RAF's night offensive against Germany. Over 7000 Lancasters were built between 1941 and 1945, and two examples survive in flying condition – one in the UK and one in Canada.**

"The bomber will always get through. The only defence is in offence, which means that you have to kill more women and children more quickly than the enemy if you want to save yourselves."
British Prime Minister Stanley Baldwin, November 10, 1932

Bombers of the Spanish Civil War

Between the two world wars in Europe, there was only one major military conflict – the Spanish Civil War fought between the Nationalists under Franco and the Republicans who fought to protect the left-wing government. The Soviet Union was quick to offer aid to the Republicans, the equipment including Polikarpov fighters and the Tupolev SB-2 bomber. Italy, under Mussolini, supported Franco by sending over 700 aircraft, including S.M.79 Sparviero and B.R.20 bombers and S.M.81 bomber-transports. The Nationalists, however, had already asked for assistance from a far more formidable ally – Germany. The Third Reich saw the Spanish Civil War as a great opportunity – it was a means of taking the world's attention away from a re-arming

> "Air power may either end war or end civilization."
> Winston Churchill, 1933

Germany, but also allowed Germany to test its troops and equipment in combat. A foothold in Spain would also allow Germany a southern launchpad for a later invasion of France.

Around 19,000 German volunteers, most of them Luftwaffe personnel, ultimately fought as part of the fighting force named the Condor Legion. Armed with Germany's latest fighter and bomber types, men and machines were tested under fire. German bombers that saw action included the Heinkel He111, Junkers Ju 52/3m and Ju 87 Stuka, and the Dornier Do17.

While the bomber aircraft of the Condor Legion were used largely in support of ground forces, they were also deployed in the strategic bombing role. While military leaders around the world considered the use of the bomber as a strategic weapon, the Germans were gaining valuable combat experience. Allegedly, Condor Legion bomber crews were initially given tourist maps to locate their targets. Despite amateurish beginnings, on April 26, 1937, the bombers of

BELOW: **The Heinkel He111 flew as part of the Condor Legion, and proved very effective against Republican forces. The He111 achieved infamy as one of the types that carried out the bombing raid against Guernica in April 1937. The aircraft pictured is a Spanish-built CASA 2.111 version.**

LEFT: **The Ju 87 Stuka dive-bomber used Spain as a testing-ground, and proved its worth to military leaders. The Stuka was more than a dive-bomber – sirens were fitted to the undercarriage to generate an ear-splitting screech intended to terrify the enemy beneath it.** BELOW: **A Condor Legion Heinkel He111-B-1, having made a forced landing after a mission.**

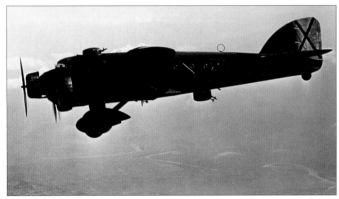

ABOVE: **The Italians supplied aircraft in support of Franco, including Savoia Marchetti S.M.81 bomber-transports. This example is pictured on a reconnaissance flight over the Ebro front.** RIGHT: **An impressive line-up of aircraft, including Ju 52s and S.M.81s at a May 1939 review of Nationalist aviation at the end of the campaign at Barajas.**

the Condor Legion attacked the small town of Guernica in northern Spain and changed the world's views of bomber aircraft forever.

For over three hours, Heinkel He111 bombers, accompanied by strafing fighters, dropped 45,000kg/ 100,000lb of high-explosive and incendiary bombs on Guernica, systematically pounding it to rubble. Over 1600 civilians, one third of the population, were killed, and almost 900 more were wounded. Seventy per cent of the town was destroyed and the fires started by the incendiaries burned for three days.

Guernica had no strategic value as a military target, but a German report at the time stated that "...the concentrated attack on Guernica was the greatest success." Guernica had been used to test a new Nazi military tactic – carpet-bombing the civilian population to demoralize the enemy. However, the effect of the attack on Guernica went far beyond the Republican forces. Guernica made some European countries fear they might be next, thus making them more responsive to German demands for capitulation.

The Spanish Civil War ended in March 1939 with the surrender of Republican forces in Madrid. The Condor Legion had been instrumental in securing victory for the Nationalists.

At the post-war Nuremberg trials, the chief of the Luftwaffe Hermann Goering said, "Spain gave me an opportunity to try out my young air force." The Blitzkrieg tactic, later used across Europe, had been refined in Spain. The 19,000 battle-hardened Luftwaffe personnel who rotated through the Condor Legion between 1936 and 1939 were soon in action over Poland, Czechoslovakia, Holland, Belgium and France – Spain had taught them well.

LEFT: **The Heinkel 111 was an effective tactical bomber, but lacked the bomb load to help the Luftwaffe pound Britain into submission.**
BELOW: **A classic wartime photograph of a Luftwaffe He111 over the River Thames and the Rotherhithe and Millwall areas of London.**

The Blitz

When Britain declared war on Germany in September 1939, Luftwaffe raids over London and elsewhere in the nation were widely expected. Large public air-raid shelters were provided, and over a million Anderson do-it-yourself shelters were distributed among those living in large towns and cities. Aware of the fate of those who had already faced the German war machine, around 13 per cent of the population left London in the days following the declaration of war, and many children were evacuated to the country. The panic subsided when the expected attacks did not come, and many of those who had left London returned.

When large-scale bombing raids came in the summer of 1940, they were directed against Royal Air Force Fighter Command as a prelude to invasion, for Hitler knew that he needed air superiority before any invasion could succeed. The success of RAF Fighter Command and the Few in what came to be known as the Battle of Britain is well documented. However, the British victory was due in no small part to a German switch in tactics – Luftwaffe raids against Fighter Command and Britain's air defence capability were largely abandoned in early September and attacks were directed at the nation's capital to erode the morale of the population. The change in tactics may have been brought about by an inept German bomber crew who, on August 24, bombed a residential area of south London apparently in error. This prompted a retaliatory attack by the RAF on the night of August 26. While the RAF raid caused little damage, Hitler was furious, and personally ordered attacks against London on September 4.

The first large-scale air raids on London targeted industrial areas and the docks. Initially these raids took place in daylight and at night, but heavy daytime losses led the Luftwaffe to restrict their attacks to darkness. At night, due to the inadequacies of British night defences at the time, the Luftwaffe were able to operate largely unmolested.

From mid-September, the Luftwaffe bombed the rest of London, including Buckingham Palace. The positive effect on British morale was considerable, uniting Britons of all classes against a common enemy. High morale among Londoners was essential when the Luftwaffe dropped 5385 tonnes/5300 tons of high explosives on London over 24 nights in September 1940.

Air raids continued most nights with up to 400 bombers dropping 406 tonnes/400 tons of high explosives and incendiaries on the capital. Although London's transport infrastructure was constantly disrupted, as were supplies of gas, electricity and water, repairs were effected swiftly to thwart the German aim of bringing chaos to the heart of their enemy. The general resilience of the population, christened the Spirit of the Blitz, meant that for the most part, London not only continued to function effectively, but was determined to fight on, even though by October 1940 around 250,000 people had been made homeless by the Blitz.

Raids on other British cities began in November 1940 and reached as far as Wales, Scotland and Northern Ireland. The Luftwaffe did however continue to make frequent visits to London. On May 10, 1941, 550 Luftwaffe bombers dropped

LEFT: Initially used in raids against Britain, Ju 87s proved to be easy meat for the Spitfires and Hurricanes of RAF Fighter Command, and they were withdrawn from operations against the UK. BELOW: Smoke billows over London, silhouetting Tower Bridge and the Tower of London, following a Luftwaffe raid on the East London Dockland on September 7, 1940.

ABOVE: An iconic image of the Battle of Britain as the Luftwaffe attempt to sweep RAF Fighter Command from the sky over England. The vapour trails were short-lived pointers to the deadly air combat taking place over southern Britain in the summer of 1940. RIGHT: Troops and police examine the wreckage of a German bomber which crashed on London's Victoria railway station during the Blitz.

more than 711 tonnes/700 tons of German bombs and thousands of incendiaries on London in what was probably the worst raid of the Blitz. Nearly 1500 people were killed and around 1800 were seriously injured in the last of the large attacks on London at this stage in the war.

On the night of November 14–15, 1940, around 500 German bombers dropped 508 tonnes/500 tons of high explosives and incendiaries on Coventry, a major industrial city. During the 10-hour onslaught, 550 people were killed, 1000 injured, and many thousands of homes were damaged or destroyed. Coventry Cathedral, left in ruins by the devastating raids, came to symbolize German aggression, and the attack on Coventry gave impetus to the planning of the very large strategic raids by Allied bombers that came later in the war, both in Europe and in Japan.

The German Blitzkrieg technique of waging war failed against Britain because the Luftwaffe was only equipped to fight tactically. The principal German bomber was the twin-engined Heinkel He111 medium-range bomber that carried a maximum bomb load of around 2277kg/5000lb over a relatively short distance. The aircraft was simply not suited for sustained attacks against targets over a long distance. Other German bombers, such as the Junkers Ju 88 and Dornier Do17, were equally unsuited to strategic bombing raids. The British and Americans, however, believed that heavy bombers could win a war. Had the Luftwaffe been equipped with large four-engined heavy bombers like those deployed by RAF Bomber Command or the US Eighth Air Force, then Germany might well have been able to bomb the population of Britain into submission.

The Dambusters

No.617 Squadron, the most famous squadron in the Royal Air Force, was formed at Scampton on March 21, 1943, under the command of Wing Commander Guy Gibson. An outstanding pilot and leader, Gibson was allowed to have his pick of crews from other squadrons to fly Lancasters on a special, highly-secret operation. Gibson himself was not told for some weeks that Operation Chastise, codename for the dams raids, involved breaching the Möhne, Eder and Sorpe Dams which held back more than 300 million tons of water vitally important to German industry.

This secret mission required a special bomb which had to be delivered in a highly unusual manner. The bomb had to be spun in the bomb bay of the aircraft at 500rpm so that when it hit the water it would "skip" across the surface rather than sink. The crew had to release the bomb while flying exactly 18.3m/60ft above the water at a speed of exactly 354kph/ 220mph. The bomb also had to impact the water at exactly 388m/425yd from the dam wall and only a 6 per cent deviation was permissible. The targets under attack were heavily defended, and the raids had to take place at night.

The first Lancaster took off from Scampton shortly before 21:30 hours on May 16, 1943, and Wing Commander Gibson's aircraft, the first to attack the Möhne Dam, released its mine at 28 minutes past midnight. Half an hour later, just after the fifth Lancaster had attacked, Gibson radioed England with the

BELOW: **This Lancaster, preserved in the UK, frequently flies commemorative fly-pasts over the Derbyshire lake that was used to train the Dambusters. The Lancasters used for the mission were specially modified to accommodate the unusual weapon and the equipment required to "spin" it.**

news that the dam had been breached. The remaining aircraft of the Möhne formation then flew on to the Eder Dam. The first two mines failed to breach the dam, but shortly before 2am, when the third Lancaster had attacked, Gibson signalled the codeword "Dinghy", indicating success with the second part of the operation. Other aircraft attacked the Sorpe and Schwelme Dams but did not succeed in breaching them. Just how low the Lancasters flew during the attack is shown by the fact that one had to turn back as it had hit the sea and lost its bomb on the journey to mainland Europe.

Of the 19 Lancasters which took off for the dams raid with their 133 crew, eight planes and 56 men did not return. Five planes crashed or were shot down en route to their targets. Two were destroyed while delivering their attacks and another was shot down on the way home. Two more were so badly damaged that they had to abandon their missions. No.617 Squadron, known from this time onwards as the "Dambusters", had become famous.

The attack had huge propaganda value and made Gibson a national hero. Gibson was awarded the Victoria Cross for bringing round his Lancaster to give covering fire to the Lancasters that were following up his attack on the Möhne Dam. Thirty-one other members of 617 Squadron were also decorated.

Severe flooding occurred where the Möhne Dam was breached. Six small electricity works were damaged and rail lines passing through the Möhne Valley were disrupted. But industrial production was not affected in the long term. When the Eder Dam broke, there were similar results. Kassel, an

ABOVE: **Guy Gibson (left) was a gifted pilot and leader who handpicked his crews for the historic dams mission. He did not survive the war but his version of the dams raids is recorded in his book "Enemy Coast Ahead".**

important arms-producing town, was reached by the flood-water, but little actual damage was done. Had the Sorpe Dam been breached, the damage would have been much greater. The potential for a major disaster was recognized by Albert Speer who commented, "Ruhr production would have suffered the heaviest possible blow."

In the short and long term, the damage done by 617 Squadron was repaired quite quickly. But the most important impact of the raid was that 20,000 men working on the Atlantic Wall had to be moved to the Ruhr to carry out repairs to the damaged and breached dams. This work was completed before the rains of the autumn appeared.

BELOW OPPOSITE AND BELOW, FROM LEFT TO RIGHT: **These stills from a film of a training flight show the spinning bomb falling from the aircraft, striking the water and then bouncing. In the last image of the sequence, pieces of the Lancaster can be seen falling away, having been knocked off by the force of the water thrown up as the bomb hit the water.**

The Mighty Eighth Air Force

On August 17, 1942, 12 Boeing B-17 Flying Fortress bombers of the 97th Bomb Group took off from Grafton Underwood in Northamptonshire, England, to attack targets in occupied France, on what was to be the first US heavy bombing mission flown from the UK in World War II.

From 1942 until the end of the war in 1945, the Eighth Air Force flew B-17 Flying Fortresses and B-24 Liberators in daylight bombing operations against Germany and Nazi-occupied Europe. At its peak strength, the Eighth Air Force could launch more than 2000 four-engine bombers and more than 1000 fighters on a single mission. For these reasons, the Eighth Air Force became known as the "Mighty Eighth".

Daytime bombing was especially hazardous, and some 27,000 men of the Eighth Air Force died on operations from UK bases – the highest casualty rate of any Allied force. The Eighth's B-17s and B-24s suffered heavy losses over Europe, especially after the bombing of Germany started in January 1943. The heavy bombers had the range to reach almost any target in Germany, but in the early months there were no Allied fighters with the range to follow and protect them. Once the Allied fighter escorts turned back, the

> "Hitler built a fortress around Europe, but he forgot to put a roof on it."
> Franklin D. Roosevelt

TOP: **This B-17F named "Hells Angels" became the first Eighth Air Force bomber to complete 25 combat missions on May 13, 1943. The famed B-17 "Memphis Belle" was the first to complete the 25 missions and return to the USA.** ABOVE: **Eighth Air Force bombers packed real teeth, as this B-17 waist gunner shows, with his 12.7mm/0.5in Browning machine-gun. A total of 305 8AF air-gunners achieved "ace" status, being credited with at least five air kills each.**

Eighth's bombers were vulnerable to attacks by German Luftwaffe fighters. During the spring, summer and autumn of 1943, Eighth Air Force losses of aircraft and aircrew sometimes reached 12 per cent for a day's raid and at one point it became statistically impossible for a bomber crewman to survive a 25-mission tour of duty. The effect that this had on morale was considerable.

When the Eighth Air Force fighters became able to escort the bombers all the way to their targets and back, the losses slowly began to drop back to what were considered to be acceptable levels, although they remained high.

The Eighth also participated in the preparation for the invasion of occupied Europe in June 1944 by bombing German missile sites and defences, and by flying special operations to support French resistance fighters and Allied ground troops. Later in the war, the Eighth also flew humanitarian missions dropping food and supplies to civilians liberated from Nazi rule.

The Mighty Eighth compiled an impressive record during World War II. Seventeen Congressional Medals of Honor went to Eighth Air Force personnel, and by the end of World War II they had been awarded a number of other medals, including 220 Distinguished Service Crosses and 442,000 Air Medals. Many more awards made to Eighth Air Force veterans after the war remain uncounted. There were 261 fighter aces (with five confirmed kills or more) in the Eighth Air Force in World War II. Thirty-one of these aces had 15 or more aircraft kills each. Another 305 enlisted gunners were also acknowledged as aces.

By the end of the war in Europe, the Eighth had fired over 100 million rounds of ammunition and dropped 703,550 tonnes/ 692,470 tons of bombs at a cost of 4162 heavy bombers and 2222 fighter aircraft lost.

The actions of the Mighty Eighth played a major role in disrupting Germany's war economy and transportation system and, ultimately, in the destruction of Nazi Germany.

ABOVE LEFT: **The G-model of the Flying Fortress, equipped with a chin turret, was able to defend itself against head-on attack – a weak spot on earlier models. Flying in box formations, the bombers would provide cover for each other against enemy fighters.** ABOVE: **B-17s raining down bombs on enemy targets.** LEFT: **The B-24 Liberator is often overshadowed by the B-17, but it was deployed in greater numbers than the Boeing bomber. This photograph taken in the summer of 1944 shows a B-24 sheathed in flames over Austria – it crashed within minutes.**

The Doolittle raid

The April 1942 air attack on Japan, launched from the aircraft carrier USS *Hornet* and led by Lieutenant Colonel James H. Doolittle, was at that point the most daring operation undertaken by the United States in the Pacific War. Though conceived as a diversion that would also boost American and Allied morale, the raid generated strategic benefits that far outweighed its limited goals.

The raid had its roots in a chance remark that it might be possible to launch twin-engined bombers from the deck of an aircraft carrier, making feasible an early air attack on Japan. On hearing of the idea in January 1942, US Fleet commander Admiral Ernest J. King and Air Forces leader General Henry H. "Hap" Arnold responded enthusiastically. Arnold assigned Doolittle to assemble and lead a suitable air group. The well-tested and proven B-25 Mitchell medium

RIGHT: **Doolittle (left) and Captain Mitscher on board the USS *Hornet* just before the historic bombing of Tokyo in April 1942.** BELOW: **The North American B-25 Mitchell was a rugged bomber that made its combat debut by sinking a Japanese submarine on December 24, 1941. The type went on to become one of the most widely used aircraft of World War II, serving with many Allied air forces.**

bomber was selected, and tests showed that it could indeed fly off a carrier while carrying bombs and enough fuel to reach and attack Japan, and then continue to friendly China.

Recruiting volunteer aircrews for the top-secret mission, Doolittle began special training for his men and modifications to their aircraft. The new carrier *Hornet* was sent to the Pacific to carry out the Navy's part of the mission, which was so secret that her Commanding Officer, Captain Mitscher, had no idea of his ship's part in the operation until just before 16 B-25s were loaded on to his flight deck. *Hornet* sailed on April 2, 1942, and headed west to be joined in mid-ocean on April 13 by USS *Enterprise*, which would provide limited air cover.

The plan called for an afternoon launch on April 18, around 643km/400 miles from Japan, but enemy vessels were met before dawn on April 18. The small enemy boats were believed to have radioed Japan with details of the American carriers heading their way, so Doolittle's Raiders had to take off immediately while still more than 965km/600 miles from their target.

Most of the 16 B-25s, each with a crew of five, attacked the Tokyo area, while some bombed Nagoya. Damage to Japanese military targets was slight, and none of the aircraft reached China, although virtually all the crews survived.

Japan's military leaders were nevertheless horrified and embarrassed by the audacious raid. The Americans had attacked the home islands once and could do it again, and so the Japanese were forced to keep more ships and aircraft in the home islands in case of further US attacks. These significant military resources could have been used against American forces as they attacked island after island while making their way closer to Japan.

Combined Fleet Commander Admiral Isoroku Yamamoto proposed that the Japanese removed the risk of any similar American raids by destroying America's aircraft carriers in the theatre. This move led the Japanese to disaster at the Battle of Midway a month and a half later.

Perhaps the most significant result of the Doolittle mission was the hard-to-quantify but very real effect that it had on American morale. The United States was finally hitting back after Pearl Harbor, and the brave men who were the Doolittle Raiders raised the confidence and morale of all Americans, civilians and military alike.

ABOVE: **The start of the Pacific War – the Japanese attack on Pearl Harbor, on December 7, 1941.** ABOVE RIGHT: **The Doolittle Raiders en route to their mission aboard the *Hornet*.** RIGHT: **An historic photograph of a B-25 leaving the deck of the *Hornet* at the start of the bombing mission over Tokyo. The raid's effects went far beyond the material damage caused by the bombs dropped that day.**

The atomic bomb raids

"Sixteen hours ago, an American airplane dropped one bomb on Hiroshima, Japan, and destroyed its usefulness to the enemy. That bomb had more power than 20,000 tons of TNT. It had more than two thousand times the blast power of the British Grand Slam, which is the largest bomb ever yet used in the history of warfare... It is an atomic bomb. It is a harnessing of the basic power of the universe." US President Harry Truman, August 6, 1945.

In late 1944, the United States began full-scale air raids on Japan, and by late spring 1945, the US 20th Air Force had destroyed or disabled many of Japan's major cities with fire-bombing raids. However, Japanese ground forces in the Pacific continued to fight, and the US military believed the death toll among US personnel would rise dramatically as the Allies moved closer to the Japanese home islands. Meanwhile, two billion US dollars had been spent and 200,000 people were working on the Manhattan Project to produce a super-weapon – the atomic bomb. After a successful test on July 16, 1945, it was decided that one instant devastating blow to a Japanese city might persuade the Japanese to surrender and save perhaps hundreds of thousands of lives on all sides.

In late 1943, Manhattan Project scientists were confident enough to tell the Army Air Forces (AAF) to begin

ABOVE: The B-29 was the world's most advanced bomber and the only aircraft in the US inventory really capable of carrying out the demanding mission. This B-29, preserved in the USA, is the only flying example of the Superfortress.
BELOW: Col. Paul Tibbets (centre, with pipe), commander of the historic mission, pictured with the ground crew of the *Enola Gay* and the aircraft on Tinian. Tibbets was a highly experienced combat pilot who had taken part in early Eighth Air Force raids from Britain. The *Enola Gay* is preserved in the USA.

preparing for the atomic bomb's use. The B-29, the world's most advanced bomber, was the obvious choice for the delivery vehicle and, under the leadership of Colonel Paul Tibbets, a hand-picked unit trained hard for one job – dropping atomic bombs.

Fifteen specially modified Boeing B-29 Superfortresses were prepared for "special weapons" delivery. The 509th Composite Group was the first USAAF bombardment group to be organized, equipped and trained for atomic warfare, needless to say under complete secrecy. Tibbets emphasized high-altitude flying, long-range navigation and the use of radar in training to prepare the crews for a high-altitude release of the bomb many miles from their base. They also worked on an escape manoeuvre that would avoid the shock wave that could damage or destroy the aircraft.

As part of the training, a 4540kg/10,000lb bomb was dropped, designed to simulate the actual "Fat Man" atomic bomb later dropped at Nagasaki. Loaded with high explosive, these were named "pumpkin" bombs because of their shape and colour. From November 1944 to June 1945, the 509th trained continually for the first atomic bomb drop. In April 1945, the group had moved to a new base on Tinian in the Mariana Islands, only 2333km/1450 miles from Tokyo.

Hiroshima was chosen as the first target, with Kokura and Nagasaki as second and third targets. The attack would occur as soon after August 2 as the weather allowed.

At 08:15 hours on August 6, B-29 *Enola Gay*, piloted by Tibbets, dropped the 4406kg/9700lb atom bomb codenamed "Little Boy" over Hiroshima.

"My God, what have we done?"
Robert Lewis, co-pilot of the *Enola Gay*, the B-29 that dropped the first atomic bomb, August 6, 1945

The devastation caused by the bomb brought no response to the demand for unconditional surrender, and conventional bombing raids continued. On August 9, B-29 *Bockscar* dropped the second and only remaining complete atom bomb in the US arsenal, codenamed "Fat Man", over Nagasaki. The primary target had been the city of Kokura, but clouds had obscured it. With fuel running low due to a fuel transfer problem, the pilot Chuck Sweeney proceeded to the secondary target, Nagasaki, a leading industrial centre. When the bomb detonated, it felt as though *Bockscar* was "being beaten with a telephone pole", said a member of the crew.

Japan surrendered unconditionally on August 14, and on August 28, US aircraft began landing the first occupation forces at Tokyo. B-29s were now dropping food, medicine and other supplies to US Allied prisoners. World War II was finally over, but the Atomic Age had dawned.

TOP: **Hiroshima photographed in March 1946, still showing the utter devastation caused by the explosion of the "Little Boy" atomic bomb on August 6, 1945. The bomb exploded 610m/2000ft above the centre of Hiroshima, and 6.5km²/4sq miles of the city were wiped out instantly. Anything beneath was turned to ashes, and only a few concrete buildings survived the blast – but in ruins.**
ABOVE: ***Enola Gay* returns to its base on Tinian following the first atomic bombing mission. Tibbets said of the raid, "...we had seen the city when we went in and there was nothing to see when we came back."** LEFT: **The mushroom cloud over Nagasaki following the detonation of the "Fat Man" atomic bomb on August 9, 1945. Japan surrendered unconditionally five days later.**

A–Z of World War Bombers

1914–45

There were no true bomber aircraft when World War I broke out, but military leaders were quick to realize the value of aircraft that could rain down destruction on their enemies from the air. While early bombing raids saw hand-held munitions tossed over the side of an aircraft, by the end of the Great War aircraft were being produced with the capacity to carry bomb loads of 800kg/ 1760lb over ranges in excess of 1000km/ 621 miles.

The specifications given to designers of new bomber aircraft in World War I were little changed by World War II, except in their magnitude. Some biplanes were still in front-line service. But by the end of World War II, bombers in service included the Boeing B-29, which had a range of 5229km/3250 miles and a top speed of 576kph/358mph. The weapons carried had changed in their destructive capacity. While the Handley Page bombers of World War I would have carried a number of 113kg/250lb bombs on a raid, the B-29 had to carry just one atomic bomb equivalent to 20,320 tonnes/20,000 tons of high explosives to destroy a city. The bomber had become a war-winning weapon.

LEFT: **Bristol Beaufort I.**

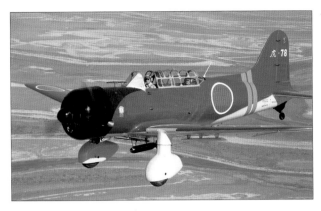

LEFT: **Although the D3A did not have a retractable undercarriage, large streamlined fairings over the fixed landing gear were used to make them more aerodynamic.**

Aichi D3A Val

First flight: January 1938
Power: One Mitsubishi 1,070hp Kinsei 44 radial piston engine
Armament: Two 7.7mm/0.303in machine-guns in upper forward fuselage plus one in rear cockpit; external bomb load of 370kg/816lb
Size: Wingspan – 14.37m/47ft 2in
Length – 10.20m/33ft 5in
Height – 3.80m/12ft 7in
Wing area – 34.9m²/375.67sq ft
Weights: Empty – 2408kg/5309lb
Maximum take-off – 3650kg/8047lb
Performance: Maximum speed – 385kph/239mph
Service ceiling – 9,300m/30,510ft
Range – 1470km/913 miles
Climb – 3000m/9845ft in 6 minutes

Aichi D3A

This two-seat low-wing monoplane dive-bomber, codenamed "Val" by the Allies, came to prominence on December 7, 1941, when a Japanese Naval Task force launched 183 aircraft, including 51 Aichi D3A-2s, from six aircraft carriers to attack Pearl Harbor's Battleship Row and other US Navy installations on the Hawaiian island of Oahu. One of the D3A-2's victims was the USS *Pennsylvania*.

The D3A first flew in January 1938, and between December 1939 and August 1945 the Aichi company built a total of 1495 aircraft in two main variants. The type D3A-1 entered service with the Imperial Japanese Navy in 1940 and was followed a year later by the D3A-2 which had the more powerful 1300hp Kinsei engine and increased fuel capacity. The D3A-2 was the main production version, with 1016 aircraft

being built by the time it became obsolete at the end of 1942. Over the following years, many were used as training aircraft, but as the war progressed and the Americans moved closer to the Japanese mainland, most of the remaining aircraft were used in kamikaze attacks against US naval ships at Leyte and Okinawa.

LEFT: **The Amiot 143 was probably the ugliest aircraft produced by a nation known for its appreciation of fine forms.**

Amiot 143

First flight: August 1934
Power: Two Gnome-Rhone 870hp Kirs 14-cylinder radial engines
Armament: Four 7.5mm/0.29in MAC 1934 machine-guns, one each in nose and dorsal turrets and fore and aft in ventral gondola; internal and external bomb load of up to 800kg/1761lb
Size: Wingspan – 24.53m/80ft 5in
Length – 18.26m/59ft 11in
Height – 5.68m/18ft 7in
Wing area – 100m²/1076.4sq ft
Weights: Empty – 6100kg/13,426lb
Maximum take-off – 9700kg/21,350lb
Performance: Maximum speed – 310kph/193mph
Service ceiling – 7900m/25,920ft
Range – 1200km/746 miles

Amiot 143

The lumbering Amiot 143 was a more powerful re-engined version of the Amiot 140 of 1931 vintage, and retained the fixed non-retractable undercarriage. This all-metal aircraft, with its distinctive two-deck fuselage, had a wing section so deep that the flight engineer could access the engines in flight. The large aerodynamic fairings that covered the wheels were 2.13m/7ft long.

Five French Groupes de Bombardement were equipped with this type in May 1940 when Germany invaded France and the Low Countries. After carrying out early raids dropping propaganda leaflets on Germany, they were restricted to night-bombing of the advancing German columns. In a rare daylight bombing raid against bridges on May 14, 1940, 12 out of 13 143s were shot down.

At the time of France's surrender, only 50 Amiot 143 aircraft remained, and these subsequently formed part of the French Vichy Air Force. By then obsolete, many were converted for use in the transport role.

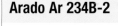

Arado Ar 234 Blitz

The origins of this type date back to a specification issued by the German Air Ministry in 1940 for a fast turbojet-powered single-seat reconnaissance aircraft. The design proposed by Arado, the Ar 234, went on to become the world's first jet-powered bomber.

The first prototype, the Ar 234V-1, first flew on June 15, 1943. and this was quickly followed by seven other prototypes, all using a launching trolley and landing skid arrangement since the aircraft's fuselage was so narrow that it could not take a conventional undercarriage. Once the aircraft reached 60m/197ft, the launch trolley was released and returned to earth on parachutes for re-use.

The third prototype, Ar 234V-3, was fitted with an ejection seat and had rocket-assisted take-off equipment

installed under the wings. During the prototype trials, the launch trolley arrangement had performed very well, but it was soon realized that the aircraft's immobility on landing would be a great disadvantage when it came to operational deployment. Turn-around times would be increased and the aircraft would be vulnerable to enemy air attack. It was therefore decided to abandon the trolley and skid, and all production aircraft had a conventional wheeled undercarriage fitted into the wider fuselage of the production B-series.

Despite being famed as the first jet bombers, early Ar 234s did serve as reconnaissance aircraft that readily avoided enemy interception. Some special examples also equipped an

Arado Ar 234B-2

First flight: June 15, 1943
Power: Two BMW 890kg/1962lb thrust 004B turbojets
Armament: External bomb load of 2000kg/4402lb
Size: Wingspan – 14.11m/46ft 3in
Length – 12.64m/41ft 5in
Height – 4.30m/14ft 1in
Wing area – 26.4m²/284.18sq ft
Weights: Empty – 5200kg/11445lb
Maximum take-off – 9850kg/21,608lb
Performance: Maximum speed – 742kph/461mph
Service ceiling – 10,000m/32,808ft
Range – 1630km/1013 miles
Climb – 6000m/19,685ft in 17.5 minutes

experimental nightfighter unit. However, Germany's fortune and the Blitz's performance soon led to its development as a bomber that entered service with the Luftwaffe in October 1944. Operated by KG76, the aircraft's first operational missions were flown against targets during the Ardennes offensive in December 1944. This jet bomber unit was very active in the early weeks of 1945 by taking part in a ten-day series of attacks against the Ludendorff bridge at Remagen, which had been captured by the Americans. The Blitz was a pioneering aircraft which was closely studied by the Allies post-war.

Armstrong Whitworth Whitley

TOP: **Z9226 was a Whitley Mk V, pictured here during its service with No.10 Squadron, Bomber Command.** ABOVE: **A Bomber Command Whitley crew prepare for another mission. Note the unusual off-centre single machine-gun in the nose turret.**

The Whitley, designed in response to Air Ministry specification B.3/34, was an all-metal twin-engined monoplane bomber with retractable landing gear, and first flew on March 17, 1936. It entered service with the RAF in March 1937, was one of the first heavy night-bombers of the RAF and the first RAF aircraft with a stressed-skin fuselage. The high incidence of the aircraft's wing gave the Whitley a distinctive nose-down flying attitude. During the "phoney war" period, the RAF's Whitley squadrons bore the brunt of leaflet dropping raids over German cities, which resulted in many losses. On March 19, 1940, Whitleys dropped the first bombs on German territory during World War II when they attacked the Hornum seaplane base on the island of Sylt. The Whitley, together with the Wellington and Hampden – lightweights by the standards of later Bomber Command "heavies" – formed the backbone of the early British bomber offensive.

Heavy losses during the winter of 1940–1 and the introduction of four-engine aircraft meant that the Whitley's front-line activities were soon restricted to Coastal Command U-boat patrol duties over the approaches to their bases along the French Atlantic coast. Coastal Command's first success using air-to-surface-vessel (ASV) radar was by a Whitley VII of No.502 Squadron against U-Boat *U-206* in November 1941.

The Whitley I was delivered to the RAF off the drawing board while the Whitley IIs were completed with two-stage superchargers for the engines. The Mark III was part of the second production run. Though similar to the II, this version

Armstrong Whitworth Whitley Mark V

First flight: March 17, 1936

Power: Two Rolls-Royce 1145hp Merlin X piston engines

Armament: One 7.7mm/0.303in machine-gun in nose turret; four in tail turret; up to 3178kg/7000lb bomb load carried in bomb bay and inner wings

Size: Wingspan – 25.6m/84 ft
Length – 21.5m/70ft 6in
Height – 4.57m/15ft
Wing area – 105.63m²/1137sq ft

Weights: Empty – 8785kg/19,350lb
Maximum take-off – 15,209kg/33,500lb

Performance: Maximum speed – 357kph/222mph
Service ceiling – 7930m/26,000ft
Range – 2654km/1650 miles
Climb – 244m/800ft per minute

ABOVE: **The famed Merlin engine did not power Whitleys until the introduction of the Mk IV. The aircraft shown here, undergoing intense but staged servicing, is a Mk III with Armstrong Siddeley Tiger engines.** RIGHT: **RAF Coastal Command operated Whitleys on maritime patrol duties. Initially standard bomber aircraft, such as that pictured, operated in the role. Later the Mk VII, specially equipped with ASV radar, could readily detect enemy vessels below.**

had a retractable ventral "dustbin" turret armed with two 7.7mm/0.303in machine-guns – this version could also carry larger bombs. The final 40 airframes of the second production run were completed as Whitley IVs with the famous Rolls-Royce Merlin engines and an increased fuel capacity.

The Mark V was similar to the Mark IV but replaced the manually operated turret with a Nash and Thompson-powered tail turret with four 7.7mm/0.303in machine-guns. As a result of combat experience, the rear fuselage of this version was also extended by 38cm/15in to improve the rear gunner's field of fire. Other changes included a revised fin shape, the addition of a leading de-icing facility and greater fuel capacity.

The Whitley VII was built specifically to serve with Coastal Command units on maritime reconnaissance duties. The VII was equipped with ASV Mk II radar and can be most readily identified from other versions by the four dorsal radar masts atop the rear fuselage, and numerous aerials carried. This model also differed by having a sixth crew member and extra fuel tankage in the bomb bay and fuselage. Compared to earlier versions with a range of 2011km/1250 miles, this version could reach distances of 3700km/2300 miles.

Earlier Bomber Command versions were phased out of front-line service from 1942, after which they were used as trainers and glider tugs – the aircraft was heavily used for training airborne troops for D-Day. During 1942–3, 15 Whitley Mk Vs were transferred to BOAC and given civil registrations to carry out Gibraltar-to-Malta supply flights. Some Whitleys served in the Fleet Air Arm until 1946 as flying classrooms to instruct on Merlin engine handling and fuel transfer.

ABOVE: **When phased out as bombers, early versions were switched to glider tug and paratroop training, thus playing a part in the success of D-Day.**

LEFT: **The Anson was one of the longest-serving RAF aircraft. This Anson bears the squadron codes of Coastal Command's No.206 Squadron.** BELOW: **Although the Anson was advanced in some ways, early versions had to be started by hand.**

Avro Anson

The origins of the Anson lay in the Avro 652 light transport airliner that served with Imperial Airways from March 1935. The 652 had been built to meet an Imperial Airways requirement for an aircraft that could transport four passengers over a series of 676km/420 mile journeys at a cruising speed greater than 209kph/130mph. Roy Chadwick, who later worked on Avro's Lancaster and early stages of the Vulcan's design, led the design team to produce what was an innovative aircraft for the time.

The Avro 652 was swiftly adapted to meet a May 1934 Air Ministry requirement for a twin-engine coastal reconnaissance aircraft. The Anson differed from its civil predecessor by having different engines, rectangular, not round, windows and also in having "teeth" in the form of a hand-operated dorsal Armstrong Whitworth turret with a 7.7mm/0.303in Lewis machine-gun. In comparative trials, the Anson was pitted against a military version of the de Havilland Dragon Rapide designed to satisfy the same RAF requirement. The Avro design's greater range and endurance impressed the Air Ministry, and a large order was placed.

The Anson represented a major breakthrough for the Royal Air Force, being the first monoplane in RAF squadron service and also the first to employ the novel retractable undercarriage, even though it was hand-operated.

The prototype first flew in 1935, and Coastal Command's No.48 Squadron at Manston was the first operational Royal Air Force Anson unit. From 1936 until the start of World War II, Ansons served in front-line squadrons of RAF Coastal Command on general reconnaissance and search-and-rescue duties. By the outbreak of war in September 1939, the RAF had 760 Mk Is equipping 10 Coastal and 16 Bomber Command squadrons, where they served as an interim aircraft until other types, such as the Armstrong Whitworth Whitley, Lockheed Hudson and Handley Page Hampden, were available.

The Anson was right in the front line of Britain's defences at the time. On September 5, 1939, an Anson of No.500 Squadron made the first attack of the war on an enemy U-boat. In June 1940, three Ansons, attacked over the Channel by nine Luftwaffe Messerschmitt Bf109s, succeeded in shooting down two and damaging one of the German fighters. Having earned its spurs, the Anson, or "Faithful Annie" as it was nicknamed in RAF service, soon settled down to the more sedate career of a trainer and light transport aircraft, although some remained with Coastal Command in the air-sea rescue role during the war years. The Commonwealth Air Training Plan of 1939 saw almost all British and Commonwealth navigators, air gunners and wireless operators trained on Ansons. Purpose-built Anson trainers had dual controls and trailing edge flaps as well as a hydraulically operated undercarriage.

By the time production ceased in 1952, Avro had made over 8000 Ansons in Britain and a further 2882 in Canada. This was one of the longest production runs of any British aircraft. In addition to the RAF, the type had been operated by 12 other air forces around the world, including those of Australia, Belgium, Estonia, Finland, Egypt and the USA.

After the war, later versions of the Anson were largely used for transport purposes, and in March 1956 the Avro Anson completed 20 years' service with the RAF, rivalling the long service of its company predecessor, the Avro 504 biplane. The official retirement of the Anson from RAF service was on June 28, 1968, when the last six Ansons on the Southern Communications Squadron were withdrawn, setting a record at the time of 32 years in RAF service.

Avro Anson Mk I

First flight: March 24, 1935

Power: Two Armstrong Siddeley 335hp Cheetah IX radials

Armament: One fixed forward-firing 7.7mm/0.303in Lewis machine-gun, plus another in dorsal turret; 163kg/360lb bomb load

Size: Wingspan – 17.22m/56ft 6in
Length – 12.87m/42ft 3in
Height – 3.99m/13ft 1in
Wing area – 43.01m²/463sq ft

Weights: Empty – 2440kg/5375lb
Maximum take-off – 3632kg/8000lb

Performance: Maximum speed – 302kph/188mph
Ceiling – 5790m/19,000ft
Range – 1062km/660 miles
Climb – 293m/960ft per minute

Avro Manchester

The twin-engine prototype Manchester, the Avro 679, was flown from Ringway (now Manchester International Airport) with Avro chief test-pilot Sam Brown at the controls for the first time on July 25, 1939. The aircraft had been designed by Avro chief designer Roy Chadwick to Air Ministry Specification P.13/36, which called for a twin-engine bomber powered by the new Rolls-Royce Vulture engine. Handley Page had also entered the competition for this Air Ministry contract with its H.P.56 project, but owing to the slow development of the Vulture engine, the company decided to change its design to a four-engine aircraft using the Rolls-Royce Merlin V-12 engine. Their project was to become the very successful Halifax.

Even though the Vulture development programme had been constantly delayed by numerous problems, Chadwick still kept faith with the troublesome new engine. In January 1940 the Air Ministry placed an order for 1200 Manchester Mk 1s, and the aircraft entered service with 5 Group Bomber Command in November 1940 as a replacement for the ageing Handley Page Hampden bomber.

The Manchester had an excellent airframe and should have been a good aircraft for Bomber Command, providing an increased bomb load capacity on existing bomber types, greater range and more defensive armament. Unfortunately, the Rolls-Royce Vulture engine was still very unreliable and also downrated on power from the original specification. As a result, the Manchester suffered a loss rate of 5.8 per cent on operational sorties, and many experienced bomber crews were also killed on training flights. This situation resulted in the Rolls-Royce Vulture engine development project being cancelled, and only 209 aircraft were delivered to the RAF bomber squadrons. Of these, 64 were lost on operations and a further 12 on training flights. The Manchester was withdrawn from service, and the last Bomber Command Manchester mission was a raid on Bremen on the night of June 25–6, 1942.

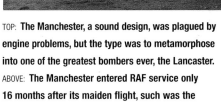
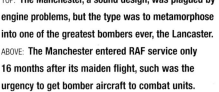

TOP: **The Manchester, a sound design, was plagued by engine problems, but the type was to metamorphose into one of the greatest bombers ever, the Lancaster.**
ABOVE: **The Manchester entered RAF service only 16 months after its maiden flight, such was the urgency to get bomber aircraft to combat units.**

Avro Manchester Mk 1

First flight: July 25, 1939
Power: Two Rolls-Royce 1760hp Vulture 24-cylinder piston engines
Armament: Eight 7.7mm/0.303in Browning machine-guns in power turrets in nose (2), mid-upper (2) and tail (4); internal bomb bay accommodating a maximum load of 4699kg/10,350lb
Size: Wingspan – 27.46m/90ft 1in
Length – 21.34m/70ft
Height – 5.94m/19ft 6in
Wing area – 105.63m²/1137sq ft
Weights: Empty – 13,362kg/29,432lb
Maximum take-off – 25,424kg/56,000lb
Performance: Maximum speed – 426kph/265mph
Ceiling – 5795m/19,000ft
Range – 2623km/1630 miles
Climb – Not available

Avro Lancaster

The Avro Lancaster became Great Britain's most famous four-engine bomber during World War II. It was developed from the ill-fated Manchester that suffered from unreliable Rolls-Royce Vulture engines. Even while the Manchester was being produced, the Avro design team, led by Chief Designer Roy Chadwick, investigated a possible four-engine replacement. The proposed four-engine Manchester Mk III, powered by Rolls Royce Merlin XX engines, was discussed with the Air Ministry on February 20, 1940. At first the proposal created little interest because most of the Merlin engine production was needed for Hurricane and Spitfire fighter aircraft. However in July 1940 the Air Ministry requested Avro to go ahead with their project and use as many Manchester components as possible in the new design.

Manchester airframe BT308 was designated project No.683 and fitted with four Rolls-Royce Merlin X engines on extended wings. This prototype model first flew on January 9, 1941 with the Manchester's triple tail fins but without ventral and dorsal turrets.

While the early handling trials were successful, a change in the tail configuration was recommended, and the original type of vertical tail surfaces were replaced by larger endplate surfaces on a wider-span tail-plane with the large central fin deleted. Exhaustive flying tests followed, and the now renamed Lancaster soon revealed its potential with excellent performances. The first production model prototype DG595 flew on May 13, 1941, and was later flown to Boscombe Down for service trials.

TOP: **The Lancaster first flew in combat on March 3, 1942, and was in the front line until the end of World War II. The Lancaster pictured is preserved in the UK by the RAF's Battle of Britain Memorial Flight.**
ABOVE: **This Mk I built by Metropolitan Vickers is being bombed-up prior to a mission.**

On June 6, 1941, Avro received a contract for 454 Lancaster Mk Is powered by four Merlin XX engines, plus two prototype Lancaster Mk IIs fitted with four Bristol Hercules VI engines.

On Christmas Eve, 1941, No.44 (Rhodesia) Squadron based at RAF Waddington in Lincolnshire received the first three production Lancaster Mk Is. The first operation with the Lancaster was carried out on March 3, 1942, when four aircraft of No.44 Squadron were detailed to lay mines in the Heligoland Bight. The Lancasters took off from Waddington at 18:15 hours and all returned safely five hours later.

The early-production Lancasters had a maximum gross take-off weight of 28,602kg/63,000lb and carried a variable bomb load up to a maximum of 6356kg/14,000lb. The bomb load mix depended upon the type of target to be attacked. For example, the bomb load for the demolition of industrial sites by blast and fire was codenamed "Cookie Plumduff" and this consisted of 1 x 1816kg/4000lb, 3 x 454kg/1000lb, plus up to six small bomb carriers loaded with 1.8kg/4lb or 13.62kg/30lb incendiaries. Later, heavier bomb loads would be carried, such as the 3632kg/8000lb Cookie, the 5448kg/12,000lb Tallboy and finally the 9988kg/22,000lb Grand Slam. The defensive armament consisted of a two-gun power turret fitted in the nose and mid-upper position plus a four-gun turret in the tail.

In February 1942 Air Chief Marshal Sir Arthur Harris became head of Bomber Command and prioritized the production of four-engine aircraft for his bomber force. Manufacturing capacity was increased by Avro but Rolls-Royce became concerned that they would not be able to satisfy the ever-increasing demand for the Merlin engines. This situation had been foreseen, and one alternative was to use a different engine – the Lancaster Mk II using the Bristol Hercules was already in the pipeline with an order for 300 placed with Armstrong Whitworth. The second solution was for the Packard Motor Corporation to manufacture the Merlin engine in the USA.

The first Lancaster Mk III powered by the Packard Merlin 28s came off the Avro production lines in August 1942. Although the Packard Merlin-powered Lancaster had almost identical performance to the Mk I, it was given the new designation because of different servicing requirements. The Packard Corporation also shipped Merlins over the Canadian border where the Victory Aircraft Company built 430 Lancaster Mk X aircraft.

With the deployment of the Mk III, a total of 7377 Lancasters were built between October 1941 and October 1945, equipping 57 RAF Bomber Command Squadrons by the end of World War II.

ABOVE: **The Lancaster was the only RAF aircraft able to carry Bomber Command's specialist ordnance such as Tallboy and Grand Slam bombs, as well as the famous "bouncing bomb".** BELOW: **The very large bomb bay of the Lancaster (the bomb bay doors are open in this photograph) enabled it to carry up to 6356kg/14,000lb of bombs. RAF Lancasters were not phased out until December 1953.**

ABOVE: **Post-war, the Lancaster was supplied to the French Navy who used the aircraft for maritime reconnaissance, as did the Royal Canadian Air Force who converted a number of Canadian-built "Lancs" for the same purpose.**

Avro Lancaster Mk I

First flight: January 9, 1941
Power: Four Rolls Royce or Packard 1460hp Merlin XX, 20 or 22s
Armament: Nose and dorsal turrets with two 7.7mm/0.303in Brownings, tail turret with four 7.7mm/0.303in Brownings; normal bomb load 6356kg/14,000lb or 9988kg/22,000lb single bomb with modifications to bomb bay
Size: Wingspan – 31.1m/102ft
Length – 21.1m/69ft 4in
Height – 5.97m/19ft 7in
Wing area – 120.45m²/1297sq ft
Weights: Empty – 16,344kg/36,000lb
Maximum take-off – 30,872kg/68,000lb
Performance: Maximum speed – 443kph/275mph at 4572m/15,000ft
Cruising speed – 322kph/200mph at 4572m/15,000ft
Service ceiling – 6706m/22,000ft
Range – 4072km/2530 miles
Climb – 6096m/20,000ft in 41 minutes, 36 seconds

Boeing B-17 Flying Fortress

In 1934 the United States Army issued a specification for a long-range, high-altitude daylight bomber for its Air Corps. The Boeing Aircraft Company responded with a prototype designated Model 299, powered by four 750hp Pratt & Whitney Hornet engines, which flew for the first time on July 28, 1935. Even though the prototype was destroyed in an accident, the project went ahead, and 13 Y1B-17s and one Y1B-17A were ordered for evaluation. After extensive trials these were designated B-17 and B-17A respectively. By the end of March 1940, the first production batch of 39 B-17Bs was delivered to the Army Air Corps, sporting a modified nose and enlarged rudder. Meanwhile, owing to the expansion of the Air Corps, a further order for 38 B-17Cs was placed. These aircraft were powered by four Wright 1200hp Cyclone engines and also featured other minor internal changes. In 1941, 20 of the B-17Cs were transferred to the RAF in England and designated Fortress Is for evaluation under combat conditions against the new generation of fast German day fighters. While the sleek four-engine all-metal Flying Fortress monoplane was unquestionably the most advanced heavy bomber in 1935, it failed with the RAF under high-altitude daylight bombing conditions by sustaining several losses, not only through enemy action but also because of mechanical and system failure.

Unfortunately for Boeing, by 1941 the B-17 had become outclassed in many respects by the new generation of medium and heavy bombers of Britain and Germany and, more importantly, that of another US aircraft company, Consolidated, whose four-engine B-24 Liberator had greater range, could carry a heavier bomb load and had better defensive armament. To retrieve the design from the verge of obsolescence, Boeing

ABOVE: **A fine air-to-air study of two B-17s preserved in flying condition in the USA. The B-17 first saw action in Europe with the Royal Air Force, who tested early models operationally. The trial was not successful because the once-advanced B-17 design had been overtaken by fighter developments.**

designed a new rear end for the aircraft. The fuselage was lengthened by 1.8m/6ft and deepened towards the rear to incorporate a tail gun position with two machine-guns projecting from the end of the fuselage. These were traversed manually and were aimed with a remote sight from the rear gunner's glazed cabin. A Sperry two-gun power turret sited in the upper fuselage aft of the pilot's cabin gave a field of fire from the horizontal plane to an all-round 75-degree elevation.

Also replacing the original under-gun emplacement just aft of the wing root came a semi-retractable rotating ball turret housing two machine-guns. In addition to the new defensive gun positions, both the hand-held guns firing through the waist openings were retained, plus the one in the radio operator's cabin. The nose armament, a single rifle-calibre machine-gun, remained unchanged, whereas all other weapons were of the larger 12.7mm/0.5in calibre, with greater range and hitting power. With this new ten-gun defensive system, the B-17E truly was a Flying Fortress.

The B-17E, with a crew of ten, was the first Flying Fortress type to see combat in the European Theatre of Operations with the US Army Air Corps. However, one defensive weakness still remained, and that was against head-on attack by high-performance German fighters armed with 20mm/0.78in cannon. A total of 512 B-17Es were built, and after further refinements the F-series entered production in April 1942.

RIGHT: **These preserved Flying Fortresses fly in formation reminiscent of the defensive boxes in which Eighth Air Force B-17s flew for their mutual protection during dangerous daylight missions.**

Over the next 18 months, 3400 B-17Fs were produced, including 61 long-range reconnaissance aircraft designated F-9s, plus another 19 delivered to RAF Coastal Command as the Fortress II.

The last production run of 86 B-17Fs were fitted with a chin-mounted power-operated Bendix turret, housing a pair of 12.7mm/0.5in machine-guns, which provided the extra fire power to help stave off the Luftwaffe frontal fighter attacks. The Bendix chin turret became a standard production item, and the type was designated B-17G. This variant started to enter service with the US Bombardment Groups in the autumn of 1943 and became the main production type, with 8680 aircraft built by the end of hostilities in Europe. Another 85 B-17Gs served with RAF Coastal Command as Fortress IIIs.

During World War II USAAF B17 Flying Fortresses flew 294,875 sorties to targets all over Europe, dropping 650,240 tonnes/640,000 tons of bombs at a cost of 4483 aircraft missing in action, plus other operational losses of 861.

RIGHT: **The B-17G model introduced the Bendix chin turret mounting two 12.7mm/0.5in machine-guns for defence against head-on attacks.**
BELOW: **Immortalized by the wartime propaganda film "Memphis Belle", many of the world's surviving B-17s – including the aircraft pictured here – came together for the filming of the 1990 blockbuster of the same name.**

Boeing B-17G Flying Fortress

First flight: July 28, 1935

Power: Four Wright 1200hp Cyclone R-1820-97 radial piston engines

Armament: Twin 12.7mm/0.5in machine-guns under nose, aft of cockpit, under centre fuselage and in tail, and single-gun mountings in side of nose, in radio operator's hatch and two waist positions; maximum bomb load 7990kg/ 17,600lb

Size: Wingspan – 31.62m/103ft 9in
Length – 22.78m/74ft 9in
Height – 5.82m/19ft 1in
Wing area – 131.92m²/1420sq ft

Weights: Empty – 13,488kg/29,710lb
Maximum take-off – 29,737kg/65,500lb

Performance: Maximum speed – 462kph/287mph
Ceiling – 10,920m/35,800ft
Range – 3220km/2000 miles
Climb – 427m/1400ft per minute

Boeing B-29 Superfortress

The B-29 Superfortress, the most advanced bomber produced during World War II, was the result of Boeing's reaction to specification XC-218, which called for a bomber with a range in excess of 8045km/5000 miles that could carry a bigger bomb load at a higher speed than the B-17B. Fortunately for Boeing, design work had been carried out on their next generation of heavy bombers over the preceding two years, and a full-scale mock-up of model 341 had been produced. This was remarkably close to specification XC-218, and so with a small amount of re-work, Boeing were able to submit their design. Three prototypes were ordered, and the first XB-29 flew on September 21, 1942. Meanwhile, a priority order for 1500 aircraft had been placed with Boeing following the Japanese attack on Pearl Harbor. The first YB-29 evaluation aircraft was delivered to the 58th Bombardment Wing in July 1943 and was followed three months later by the first batch of B-29-BW production aircraft. The Superfortress had many advanced features, including remotely controlled gun turrets and a partly pressurized fuselage.

RIGHT: **The B-29 was not used in Europe during World War II, instead being limited to the Pacific theatre.** BELOW: **The B-29 was a major technological leap forward for the USAAF, bringing huge increases in performance with it.**

At the end of 1943 the decision was made to use only the B-29 against the Japanese in the Pacific theatre. In the spring of 1944 the two fully equipped bombardment wings were deployed to bases in India and south-west China. The first bombing mission was flown on June 5 against Japanese targets in Thailand, and was followed a few days later by raids against the Japanese mainland. With the establishment of five air bases on the Mariana Islands in March 1944, the B-29 bombardment wings were able to mount a sustained bombing campaign against mainland Japan. It was from one of these bases in August 1945 that B-29 *Enola Gay* dropped the first atomic bomb on the city of Hiroshima, followed three days later by B-29 *Bockscar* dropping a second on Nagasaki. The Boeing bomber played a vital role in the defeat of Japan, who surrendered on August 14, five days after the Nagasaki raid.

**Boeing B-29
Superfortress**

First flight: September 21, 1942

Power: Four Wright 2200hp R-3350-57 radial
engines

Armament: Four-gun turret over nose, two-gun
turrets under nose, over and under rear
fuselage, all with machine-guns of 12.7mm/
0.5in calibre, plus one 20mm/0.78in and two
12.7mm/0.5in guns in tail; up to 9080kg/
20,000lb bomb load

Size: Wingspan – 43.05m/141ft 3in
Length – 30.18m/99ft
Height – 9.01m/29ft 7in
Wing area – 161.27m²/1736sq ft

Weights: Empty – 31,843kg/70,140lb
Maximum take-off – 56,296kg/124,000lb

Performance: Maximum speed – 576kph/358mph
Ceiling – 9695m/31,800ft
Range – 5229km/3250 miles
Climb – 7625m/25,000ft in 43 minutes

ABOVE: **The B-29's performance and large bomb load made it the only choice for the delivery of the atomic bombs to Japan.** RIGHT: **The B-29 was used extensively during the Korean War, initially in support of ground troops but then more appropriately as a strategic bomber. Back in the USA, the Superfortress was the main aircraft of the fledgling Strategic Air Command.** BELOW: **The Soviet copy of the B-29, the Tu-4, influenced Soviet bomber design for years after they "acquired" it at the end of World War II.**

The B-29 may be famous or infamous for the atomic bomb raids, but the many conventional, largely incendiary, bombing raids carried out by the Superfortresses against Japan ultimately destroyed the centres of a number of large Japanese cities.

After the war, the B-29 became the mainstay of the newly formed USAF Strategic Air Command, and later saw continuous action during the three-year Korean War. Initially used in a tactical bomber role to halt the North Korean ground advance, the USAF B-29s were soon deployed in the role for which they were made – strategic bombing. Operating from bases in Japan, raids were carried out against industrial targets in North Korea.

The basic B-29 design underwent a number of modifications over the years. These variants included the SB-29 for air-sea rescue, the TB-29 trainer and the WB-29

tanker. The Royal Air Force operated the aircraft as the Washington, with 88 ex-USAF examples in service from 1950. Most were returned to the USA in 1954, but some remained in Bomber Command service until 1958.

The Soviet Union managed to produce a copy of the B-29, which was named the Tu-4 in Soviet service. These unlicensed copies were based on US aircraft which fell into Soviet hands at the end of World War II. In a programme unparalleled in ingenuity and audacity, the Soviet Union ultimately produced over 300 of their version. The Soviet Union's post-war atomic bomber fleet was therefore directly related to the three US B-29s which had originally made emergency landings on Soviet territory following bombing missions over Japan. America had given the Soviet Union the aircraft that could have been turned on the USA.

LEFT: **The Bre.14 replaced older types in front-line service from mid-1917. The type often attacked deep behind enemy lines.**

Breguet Bre.14

The prototype of this highly advanced two-seat light-bomber biplane made its first flight in November 1916, only six months after Breguet's chief engineer Louis Vuillierme began the design. The pilot was Louis Breguet, such was the significance and advanced nature of the aircraft. It was revolutionary for a French combat aircraft, having its engine and propeller at the front and, perhaps most impressively, it was made principally of lightweight Duralumin.

The Bre.14 A.2 production aircraft entered service with the Aeronautique Militaire in the spring of 1917 on the Western Front, and soon established a reputation among French aircrew for being robust and reliable. The principal bomber version used by France's strategic bomber force during World War I was the Bre.14 B.2.

By the end of World War I, orders for nearly 5500 Bre.14s had been placed with the Breguet aircraft manufacturing

company. The aircraft had been so successful after its introduction during the war that by the time the production line closed down in 1926, the total number of aircraft manufactured had reached 8000.

Post-war, it served in a number of roles such as light transport and air ambulance, and the type also pioneered mail routes in French equatorial Africa.

LEFT: **The Bre.19 was well used by Spain in the 1920s and early '30s.**

Breguet Bre.19

This aircraft, which had substantial amounts of aluminium alloy in its structure at an early stage in aircraft design, was built as a reconnaissance/bomber successor to Breguet's Bre.14 of World War I. It flew for the first time in March 1922 and, as a measure of progress, weighed the same as its Breguet predecessor but could carry a payload that was up to 80 per cent greater.

The Breguet company were excellent publicists and had the Bre.19 set countless world records to prove what an effective combat aircraft it was. As a result, in addition to use by the French, the aircraft was widely exported and was operated by nine other air forces. Licence-built versions were produced in Turkey, Belgium, Yugoslavia, Greece, Japan and Spain. Both sides of the

Spanish Civil War used the Bre.19 and the Chinese used the type against the Japanese in Manchuria. Greek Bre.19s were used against invading Italians in October 1940.

Breguet 691/693

The Breguet 690 series of military aircraft stemmed from a 1934 specification for a three-seat heavy fighter, which led to the Bre.690. The prototype twin-engine fighter's performance so impressed that, with war clouds gathering, the Bre.691 light attack variant (with Hispano-Suiza engines), which first flew in 1937, was swiftly put into production. This differed from the fighter version in having a bomb bay in which to carry 400kg/880lb of bombs. One hundred examples of the light bomber were ordered, but before they were all built, a new and improved version, the 693 powered by Gnome-Rhone engines, had appeared. The Bre.695 had American Pratt & Whitney Twin Wasp Junior engines. By the Fall of France, almost three hundred examples of all marks had made it to front-line units. Two French Air Force Groups GBA I/54 and II/54 were first to become fully equipped with the Bre.693. The type made its operational debut on May 12, 1940, attacking advancing German troop columns. Ten of the eleven 693s sent on the mission were destroyed. The crews battled on in spite of the overwhelming and more capable opposition, but

suffered heavy losses against the superior German single-engine fighters. By June 24, 1940, almost half of the Bre.693s in service were lost in the course of over 500 sorties in defence of their country.

The Vichy air force took over the remaining machines, and many of these were in turn seized by the Luftwaffe, who stripped the engines out to power some of their own aircraft. A number were passed on to Italy, who used the aircraft for operational training from 1942–3.

Breguet Bre.693 AB2

First flight: October 25, 1939
Power: Two 700hp Gnome-Rhone 14M Mars 14-cylinder radial engines
Armament: One 20mm/0.78in cannon and two 7.5mm/0.29in fixed forward-firing machine-guns, three 7.5mm/0.29in machine-guns fixed and obliquely rearward firing, plus one trainable; internal bomb load of 400kg/880lb
Size: Wingspan – 15.36m/50ft 5in
    Length – 9.67m/31ft 8in
    Height – 3.19m/10ft 5in
    Wing area – 28.8m²/310sq ft
Weights: Empty – 3010kg/6625lb
    Maximum take-off – 5500kg/12,105lb
Performance: Maximum speed – 475kph/295mph
    Service ceiling – 8500m/27,885ft
    Range – 1350km/839 miles
    Climb – 4000m/13,120ft in 7 minutes, 12 seconds

ABOVE, LEFT AND BELOW: **The Bre.690 fighter from which the bomber variants were developed. The ground-attack version had different engines and a bomb bay. Breguet pilots fought bravely against invading German forces, but were swiftly overwhelmed.**

Bristol Blenheim

When the Bristol Blenheim bomber entered RAF service in 1937, it represented a huge leap forward for the service – the Mk I Blenheim was considerably faster than the 290kph/180mph Hind biplane it replaced and could outrun most contemporary fighters, many of which were biplanes. Initially developed as the Type 142, a fast eight-seat passenger plane, the aircraft that became the three-seat Bristol Blenheim bomber flew for the first time in April 1935. Britain First was the name given to the Type 142, which had been ordered by newspaper tycoon Lord Rothermere, who wanted a fast executive transport.

In August 1935 the Air Ministry issued Specification B28/35 covering the conversion of the aircraft to the bomber role, and this was designated Type 142M.

Major modifications followed, including raising the wing from a low to a mid-wing position to allow room for the internal bomb bay. The nose section was also redesigned to accommodate both pilot and observer/bomb-aimer. The third member of the crew was a mid-upper gunner, who was housed in a power-operated dorsal turret with a 7.7mm/0.303in Lewis machine-gun. The pilot could also fire a Browning 7.7mm/0.303in, which was installed in the port wing leading edge.

The Air Ministry placed an initial order for 150 Blenheim Mk Is in September 1935. This was followed with a second order in December 1936 for another 434 aircraft, after a series of successful trials. In March of the following year,

TOP: **Considered to be something of a forgotten bomber, the Blenheim gave the Royal Air Force a bomber aircraft with a performance that was superior to many fighters of the time.** ABOVE: **Over 1000 Blenheims were in service when war broke out, and it was a No.139 Squadron Blenheim that was first to fly over Germany on September 3, 1939.**

Wyton-based No.114 (Hong Kong) Squadron of 2 Group Bomber Command became the first RAF squadron to be equipped with the Blenheim Mk I. A total of 1134 Mk Is were built, with 1007 being on RAF charge by August 1939. This hot-rod bomber brought much interest from overseas customers, and export versions were supplied to Greece, Finland, Turkey, Romania, Lithuania and Yugoslavia.

By the start of World War II, the Mark I had been largely replaced by the Mark IV in UK-based RAF bomber units. The Blenheim Mk IV was basically a Mk I airframe with two Bristol Mercury XV radial engines fitted with de Havilland three-blade variable-pitch propellers. It also had a redesigned and enlarged nose and extra internal fuel tanks.

At the outbreak of war in September 1939, Royal Air Force bomber squadrons had 197 Blenheim Mk IVs on strength. On September 3, a Blenheim IV of Wyton-based No.139 Squadron became the first RAF aircraft of World War II to cross the German border, while flying a reconnaissance mission. On the next day, Blenheims of Nos.107 and 110 Squadrons took part in the RAF's first offensive operation of the war, when they unsuccessfully attacked German naval units in the Elbe Estuary. While at least three bombs struck the pocket Battleship *Admiral Scheer*, they failed to explode. No.107 Squadron lost four of its five aircraft on the raid, and these were Bomber Command's first casualties of World War II.

ABOVE: **This No.110 Squadron Blenheim IV sustained damage in air combat, and had to be patched before its next mission.**

The defensive shortcomings of the Blenheim soon became apparent when the type suffered heavy losses while taking part in anti-shipping operations in the North Sea. The armament was subsequently increased to five machine-guns. In all, 1930 Mk IVs were built in the UK. Most of No.2 Group Blenheims were replaced in 1941 by the Douglas Boston and the de Havilland Mosquito.

The final British-built version of the Blenheim was the Mk V. Over 940 were built, the majority being the VD tropical variant. These were shipped out to North Africa to support the Eighth Army in the Western Desert but again, the Blenheims suffered appalling combat losses against the Messerschmitt Bf109s and were soon replaced by US-supplied Baltimores and Venturas.

In Canada, the Fairchild Aircraft Company built 676 Blenheims for the Royal Canadian Air Force, and these versions were designated the Bolingbroke Mk I to Mk IV. Finland operated the Blenheim until 1956.

RIGHT: **Blenheim IVs manned by Free French crews saw considerable action in North Africa.** BELOW: **The Blenheim was a versatile aircraft that achieved combat success in the day- and nightfighter as well as the bomber role. The aircraft pictured here is a Mark I nightfighter from RAF Squadron No.141.**

Blenheim Mk I 🇬🇧

First flight: June 25, 1936

Power: Two Bristol 920hp Mercury XV radial engines

Armament: One 7.7mm/0.303in Browning machine-gun in leading edge of port wing, one 7.7mm/0.303in Vickers machine-gun in dorsal turret; maximum internal bomb load of 454kg/1000lb

Size: Wingspan – 17.7m/58ft 1in
Length – 12.11m/39ft 9in
Height – 3m/9ft 10in
Wing area – 43.57m²/469sq ft

Weights: Empty – 3677kg/8100lb
Maximum take-off – 5675kg/12,500lb

Performance: Maximum speed – 428kph/266mph
Service ceiling – 8320m/27,280ft
Range – 1810km/1125 miles
Climb – 469m/1540ft per minute

Bristol Beaufighter

The Beaufighter came about when the Bristol company simply proposed a versatile, heavily armed aircraft that they thought the Royal Air Force needed. Using major elements of the Beaufort torpedo bomber already in production, the two-seat Beaufighter was produced quickly and joined front-line squadrons at the height of the Battle of Britain in 1940, only 13 months after the prototype first flew. Day fighter versions saw action in the Western Desert and Malta, while RAF Coastal Command also used the "Beau" to great effect, particularly over the Bay of Biscay against Junkers Ju 88s.

The development of combat aircraft relies entirely on the engines available to power the aeroplanes, and it was the improvements to the Bristol Hercules that led to the Beaufighter's development in a host of different roles. More power allowed designers to add more weight to the aircraft in the form of new weaponry, equipment, armour or fuel.

There were two significant Beaufighter developments in 1942 – a trial torpedo installation succeeded, and the type was experimentally and successfully armed with rocket projectiles.

By late 1942, Mk VICs were being completed with torpedo-carrying gear. The Beaufighter was now able to carry and launch a large torpedo (the British 45.7cm/18in or the US 57.2cm/22.5in) against shipping, and the first "Torbeau" unit

TOP: **The Beaufighter T.F. Mk X was a purpose-designed torpedo-carrying version that saw considerable RAF Coastal Command service.**

ABOVE: **T.F. Xs of No.404 Squadron RCAF, which formed part of the Banff Strike Wing in Scotland, carrying out sweeps against enemy shipping in the North Sea.**

was No.254 Squadron based at North Coates. Equipped with Mk VIC torpedo-fighters, the squadron first attacked enemy shipping with the new weapon on April 18, 1943. The Beaufort was soon phased out in favour of the new-found British torpedo-bomber.

The VIC was gradually replaced in Coastal Command service by a new purpose-designed torpedo-bomber version, the Beaufighter T.F. Mk X. This dedicated torpedo-bomber, powered by 1770hp Hercules XVII engines, was probably the best British anti-shipping aircraft in service in the later stages of World War II. The Hercules Mk XVII was developed to optimize the Beaufighter for low-level missions, and achieved

peak power at just 152m/500ft. Dive brakes were also soon introduced as an aid in low-level attacks. The Mk X was the main production variant of the Beaufighter, with over 2200 produced. Normally flying with a crew of two, a third crew member could be carried to assist with torpedo-aiming. Using special equipment including a radio altimeter, the Beaufighter could make precision low-level, wave-top height attacks with torpedoes or rockets. Mk Xs ultimately carried the A.I. Mk VIII radar, adapted for use against surface targets, housed in the tell-tale "thimble-nose" radome. The Beaufighter X was an extremely effective anti-shipping aircraft, scouring the waters around Britain for German shipping. In March 1945, aircraft of Nos.236 and 254 Squadrons sank five German U-boats in just two days.

Beaufighters were also heavily used by Australian units on anti-shipping missions. Australia produced their own Beaufighter Xs, some 364 in total, which were known as T.F. Mk 21s. Powered by the Hercules XVIII, the T.F.21s entered service in 1944 and played a key role in the Royal Australian Air Force's support for the Allied advance into the East Indies. These Beaufighters' high-speed, low-level attacks caused the Japanese to nickname them "Whispering Death".

Post-war, a number of Beaufighters remained in RAF service, mainly in the Far East where they retired from front-line duties in 1950. Thirty-five RAF Beaufighters were converted for use as target tugs. Designated T.T.10, these aircraft served in the UK, Middle East and Far East until 1960.

ABOVE RIGHT: **The Beaufighter was originally conceived as a multi-role aircraft, and fighter versions, like the IIF pictured, appeared during the Battle of Britain.**
RIGHT AND BELOW: **When the Beaufighter was equipped for carrying a torpedo later in the war, it became the best British anti-shipping aircraft of the time. Note the four cannon on the underside of the nose.**

Bristol Beaufighter T.F. Mk X

First flight: July 17, 1939
Power: Two Bristol 1770hp Hercules XVII 14-cylinder air-cooled radials
Armament: Four 20mm/0.78in cannon, six 7.7mm/0.303in machine-guns, one 7.7mm /0.303in machine-gun in dorsal position; one 726kg/1600lb or 965kg/2127lb torpedo, two 227kg/500lb bombs, eight 76.2mm/3in rocket projectiles
Size: Wingspan – 17.63m/57ft 10in
Length – 12.7m/41ft 8in
Height – 4.82m/15ft 10in
Wing area – 46.73m²/503sq ft
Weights: Empty – 7082kg/15,600lb
Maximum take-off – 11,440kg/25,200lb
Performance: Maximum speed – 512kph/318mph
Service ceiling – 4572m/15,000ft
Range – 2366km/1470 miles
Climb – 1524m/5000ft in 3 minutes, 30 seconds

Consolidated B-24 Liberator

With the growing possibility of war erupting in Europe, in 1939 the US Army Air Corps expressed an interest in the Consolidated Aircraft Corporation's ideas for a new four-engine, long-range, high-flying heavy bomber. As a result, a contract for one prototype was placed with the Company in March 1939, and the aircraft was designated the XB-24. The flying surfaces that were the bases of the XB-24 design had been proven in the 1930s with Consolidated's PBY flying boat. The prototype construction advanced quickly over the next few months, and the aircraft took off on its maiden flight from Lindbergh Field, California, on December 29, 1939. It was powered by four 1200hp Pratt & Whitney R-1830-33 radial engines and could carry 3632kg/8000lb of bombs in its capacious fuselage. For defensive armament it had six hand-operated 7.7mm/0.303in Browning machine-guns. The B-24 was the first American heavy bomber with a tricycle undercarriage.

Seven pre-production YB-24 aircraft, ordered for US Army Air Corps evaluation, were soon coming off the San Diego assembly line in early 1941. These aircraft were re-designated XB-24Bs because they were fitted with Pratt & Whitney 1200hp R-1830-41 engines and General Electric B-2 turbo superchargers for high-altitude flight. Other modifications included an increase to the tail span of 0.6m/2ft. The first nine production B-24A Liberators were delivered to the USAAC in May 1941. These were quickly followed by a further development batch of nine aircraft designated B-24Cs, which differed from earlier versions by having three power turrets.

TOP: **Often overshadowed by the B-17, the B-24 was in fact produced in greater numbers than any other bomber ever.** ABOVE: **Liberator IIIs (B-24Ds) stationed at Aldergrove in Northern Ireland, April 1943. Note the aerials fixed to the port wing and nose.**

Further modifications followed before the first main production model, the B-24D, started to be delivered to the various Army Air Corps Bombardment Groups. This variant had a take-off weight increased to 25,424kg/56,000lb and was powered by Pratt & Whitney R-1830-43 engines, giving a top speed of 487kph/303mph at 7625m/25,000ft. Armament was now ten 12.7mm/0.50in machine-guns and a bomb load of 3995kg/8800lb. Range was also increased by 1046km/650 miles, giving a total range of 4586km/2850 miles.

Consolidated B-24D Liberator

First flight: December 29, 1939

Power: Four Pratt & Whitney 1200hp R-1830-65 radial engines

Armament: Two gun turrets in nose, tail, upper fuselage aft of cockpit and under centre fuselage, and single manual guns in waist (beam) positions, totalling 10 12.7mm/0.5in machine-guns; normal bomb load of 3995kg/8800lb

Size: Wingspan – 33.35m/110ft
Length – 20.47m/67ft 2in
Height – 5.49m/18ft
Wing area – 97.36m²/1048sq ft

Weights: Empty – 15,436kg/34,000lb
Maximum take-off – 29,510kg/65,000lb

Performance: Maximum speed – 467kph/290mph
Service ceiling – 8540m/28,000ft
Range – 3220km/2000 miles
Climb – 6100m/20,000ft in 22 minutes

TOP: **Post-war, the B-24 was used by other nations. This is a Royal Canadian Air Force B-24.** ABOVE LEFT: **This B-24, Diamond Lil is preserved in the USA by the Commemorative (formerly Confederate) Air Force as a tribute to the aircrew who made the ultimate sacrifice in defence of freedom.** ABOVE: **In RAF service, the B-24G was designated Liberator G.R.V.**

In September 1942, the 93rd Bombardment Group became the first B-24D bombardment group to join the Eighth Air Force in England. A month later, the 44th BG arrived in the UK, also equipped with B-24s. By the end of the war in Europe, 3800 Liberators had been accepted by the Eighth Air Force. Of these, almost a third were lost in action over enemy territory.

In all, five production plants produced 19,256 Liberators between May 1941 and the end of hostilities in 1945. The Ford Motor Company, using mass-production techniques perfected for the automobile industry, built 6792 at its Willow Run plant alone.

Although the B-24 was more technologically advanced than the B-17, it is often eclipsed in history by the Boeing bomber. The facts are however quite clear – the B-24 was produced in greater numbers than any bomber in aviation history.

In August 1943, B-24s carried out one of the most famous USAAF bombing raids of World War II. Fifty-six out of

179 bombers were lost during the mission, a daring low-level attack on the Romanian oil fields, which supplied one-third of the Third Reich's high-octane fuel. Only the Liberator could reach these targets from the nearest friendly airfields in North Africa.

France had ordered 120 Liberators, but fell to the Germans in 1940 before the aircraft were delivered. Royal Air Force Coastal Command was quick to appreciate the long range of the B-24, and took over the French order. The first RAF Liberator took to the air in January 1941. The Liberator played a key role in the RAF's war against German U-boats in the Battle of the Atlantic.

Consolidated PBY-5A Catalina

The Consolidated Aircraft Corporation received a contract for a prototype flying boat from the US Navy in February 1928. The aircraft was designated XPY-1, and was designed for alternative installations of either two or three engines. However, it was the initial configuration that ultimately evolved into the most outstanding monoplane flying boat of the 1930s, the PBY Catalina.

The contract for the construction of the PBY prototype was issued to Consolidated in October 1933, and the aircraft flew for the first time in March 1935. Aircraft were delivered to the US Navy's Patrol Squadrons from October 1936. As part of a training exercise and also to demonstrate the aircraft's long-range endurance capabilities, Patrol Squadron VP-3 flew a non-stop round-trip mission from San Diego, California, to the Panama Canal Zone in 27 hours, 58 minutes, covering a distance of 5297km/3292 miles.

The PB1s were powered by 850hp Pratt & Whitney R-1830-64 engines, but in 1937 the engines were upgraded to 1000hp, and 50 aircraft were ordered, designated PB-2s. The third variant, the PB-3, was delivered to the Soviet Union in 1938 along with a manufacturing licence. The Soviet PB-3 was powered by two Russian-built 950hp M87 engines, and designated GST. The PB-4 variant also appeared in 1938 with large mid-fuselage blister observation and gun positions.

In April 1939, the US Navy ordered a prototype amphibious version that could land on water or land (with a retractable undercarriage), designated XPBY-5A. After service evaluation

TOP AND ABOVE: **The Royal Air Force made extensive use of the Catalina during World War II, having first evaluated the type in July 1939. The aircraft shown at the top of the page is in fact a Canso, the amphibious version which could operate from land or sea thanks to a retractable undercarriage.**

tests, orders were placed by the US Navy. The Royal Air Force had already shown interest in the type, aware of the gathering war clouds in Europe and the need to patrol British waters far from land. One aircraft was flown over from the USA for RAF evaluation, and as soon as war was declared 30 examples of the amphibious version were ordered. These were delivered to the RAF in early 1941 and were in service almost immediately, named the Catalina by the British. The US Navy also adopted the name Catalina in 1942. During a patrol on May 26, 1941,

ABOVE: **US Navy Catalina amphibians (PBY-5As) tied down at their Aleutian bases, World War II.** RIGHT: **RAF Catalinas operated in the Atlantic, Mediterranean and the Indian Ocean, and took part in the protection of Arctic convoys while based in Russia.**

LEFT: **The PBY was the most numerous and the most successful flying boat of World War II. It entered US Navy service in 1936 and equipped 21 patrol squadrons by the start of the war.** BELOW: **The Catalina's ingenious retractable floats became the aircraft's wingtips when retracted.**

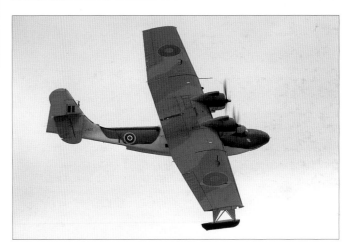

a Catalina of No.209 Squadron operating from Castle Archdale in Northern Ireland spotted the German battleship *Bismarck* once Royal Navy ships had lost the enemy ship.

The RAF had 650 Catalinas, and many served in the Atlantic. Two Royal Air Force Catalina pilots who operated in the Atlantic were awarded the Victoria Cross for gallant attacks on German submarines in the open sea. British "Cats" also operated in Ceylon and Madagascar patrolling the Indian Ocean, while aircraft operating from Gibraltar were on station for the 1942 Allied landings in North Africa. The last U-boat sunk by RAF Coastal Command was destroyed by a No.210 Squadron Catalina on May 7, 1945.

The PBY-5A variant was used widely during World War II by a number of countries. Canadian-built versions of the flying boat were also produced, and were known as "Cansos" by the Royal Canadian Air Force. Further development of the Catalina led to the fitting of more powerful 1200hp engines, revised armament and search radar equipment. By the end of production in 1945, over 4000 Catalinas had been made, making it the most-produced flying boat in history.

Catalinas were operated by many air arms around the world, including Australia, Brazil, France, the Netherlands, New Zealand, South Africa and the Soviet Union. A number remain in civilian use today, and are popular attractions at air shows.

Consolidated PBY-5 Catalina

First flight: March 1935
Power: Two Pratt & Whitney 1200hp R-1830-92 Twin Wasp 14-cylinder radial engines
Armament: Two 12.7mm/0.5in machine-guns in bow turret and one in each beam blister, one 7.62mm/0.3in machine-gun in ventral tunnel; war load of up to 1816kg/4000lb of bombs, mines or depth charges, or two torpedoes
Size: Wingspan – 31.7m/104ft
Length – 19.45m/63ft 10in
Height – 6.15m/20ft 2in
Wing area – 130m²/1400sq ft
Weights: Empty – 9493kg/20,910lb
Maximum take-off – 16,080kg/35,420lb
Performance: Maximum speed – 288kph/2135mph
Ceiling – 4480m/14,700ft
Range – 4095km/2545 miles
Climb – 189m/620ft per minute

Curtiss SB2C Helldiver

The Curtiss SB2C was the second Curtiss US naval aircraft to be called Helldiver, but shared little but a name with the earlier aircraft. The Helldiver is another aircraft whose contribution to the final Allied victory is often underestimated. Said to be a handful at low speeds, the two-man Helldiver first flew in December 1940 but did not see action until November 1943 when it took part in a carrier strike against Rabaul. The Helldiver became the most successful Allied dive-bomber of World War II, and certainly made a major contribution to the successful outcome of the war in the Pacific. The aircraft had good range, making it a very useful weapon for action in the great expanse of the Pacific. The aircraft packed a significant punch and could carry 454kg/1000lb of bombs under its wings, while a torpedo or further 454kg/1000lb could be carried in the internal bomb bay.

Later improvements to this already more than capable combat aircraft included an uprated Wright Cyclone engine and hardpoints for carrying rocket-projectiles.

The Helldiver saw considerable action in the battles of the Philippine Sea and Leyte Gulf, and played a significant part in the destruction of the Japanese battleships *Yamato* and *Musashi*. As the Allies moved towards the Japanese home islands, Helldivers were active in the Inland Sea and helped deal the deathblow to the Japanese Navy.

Post-war, Helldivers were the only bombers in the US Navy, and continued to equip USN units until 1948, when the Douglas Skyraider was introduced.

Other post-war operators of the Helldiver included the Italian, Greek and Portuguese navies. Helldivers fought on with the French Navy and were used by them in Indo-China. Thailand took delivery of six Helldivers in 1951, and retired the aircraft in 1955.

TOP AND ABOVE: **After an unimpressive service debut, the Helldiver became the standard US Navy "scout-bomber" for the remainder of World War II.**

Curtiss SB2C-4 Helldiver

First flight: December 18, 1940

Power: One Wright 1900hp Wright R-2600-20 Cyclone radial engine

Armament: Two 20mm/0.78in cannon in wings, two 7.62mm/0.3in machine-guns in rear cockpit; 454kg/1000lb of bombs or a torpedo carried internally, plus an additional 454kg/1000lb of bombs and rocket projectiles carried under wings

Size: Wingspan – 15.16m/44ft 9in
Length – 11.17m/36ft 8in
Height – 4.01m/13ft 2in
Wing area – 39.2m²/422sq ft

Weights: Empty – 4788kg/10,547lb
Maximum take-off – 7543kg/16,616lb

Performance: Maximum speed – 434kph/270mph
Service ceiling – 8875m/29,100ft
Range – 1987km/1235 miles
Climb – 549m/1800ft per minute

LEFT: **DH4s stationed in France during World War I.**

de Havilland/Airco DH4

de Havillland/Airco DH4

First flight: August 1916

Power: Various, but typically one Rolls-Royce 250hp Eagle VIII in-line piston engine

Armament: Two fixed forward-firing 7.7mm/0.303in Vickers machine-guns and two in rear cockpit; provision for 209kg/460lb of bombs

Size: Wingspan – 12.92m/42ft 4in
Length – 9.35m/30ft 8in
Height – 3.35m/11ft
Wing area – 40.32m²/434sq ft

Weights: Empty – 1083kg/2387lb
Maximum take-off – 1575kg/3472lb

Performance: Maximum speed – 230kph/143mph
Ceiling – 6710m/22,000ft
Endurance – 3 hours, 45 minutes
Climb – 1830m/6000ft in 4 minutes, 50 seconds

The DH4 was arguably the most successful light bomber to see action during World War I. The biplane was designed by Geoffrey de Havilland in response to a 1914 War Office requirement for a two-seat day bomber for service with the Royal Flying Corp (RFC) and Royal Navy Air Service (RNAS). Some have compared the aircraft's versatility in World War I to that of its de Havilland successor, the twin-engine Mosquito, whose many applications in World War II are well documented.

The DH4 was originally designed around the 200hp Beardmore-Halford-Pullinger engine. However, there were many development problems with the new engine, so no fewer than seven different engine types were fitted to production aircraft. Various sub-contractors to de Havilland built 1449 aircraft in the UK and in the USA a further 4846 were produced by three US companies. These US models were powered mainly by the 400hp Packard Liberty engine. The DH4 entered front-line service in 1917.

LEFT: **This DH9A, E8673, was built by the Aircraft Manufacturing Co. Ltd.**

de Havilland/Airco DH9A

First flight: July 1917 (DH9)

Power: One Packard 420hp Liberty 12 V-type piston engine

Armament: One fixed forward-firing 7.7mm/ 0.303in Vickers machine-gun and one or two 7.62mm/0.3in Lewis machine-guns in rear cockpit; provision for 299kg/660lb of bombs on external pylons

Size: Wingspan –14.01m/45ft 11in
Length – 9.22m/30ft 3in
Height – 3.45m/11ft 4in
Wing area – 45.22m²/486.7sq ft

Weights: Empty – 1270kg/2800lb
Maximum take-off – 2108kg/4645lb

Performance: Maximum speed – 198kph/123mph
Ceiling – 5105m/16,750ft
Endurance – 5 hours, 15 minutes
Climb – 1980m/6500ft in 8 minutes, 55 seconds

de Havilland/Airco DH9A

The DH9 was derived from the successful DH4, and first entered Royal Flying Corps service with No.103 Squadron in December 1917. The following March, it went into action on the Western Front with No.6 Squadron, but the engine was found to be underpowered. With a full bomb load of 299kg/660lb mounted on external pylons, it could only climb to around 4575m/15,000ft, which was 2135m/ 7000ft lower than the DH4 it replaced. There was also a very high rate of engine failure during bombing operations.

The disappointing performance was found to be entirely due to the problematic BHP engine, which only developed 230hp instead of the anticipated 300hp. In order to overcome the problem, the BHP engine was replaced by the 420hp Packard Liberty engine. These models, designated DH9A, went on to be some of the finest bomber aircraft of World War I.

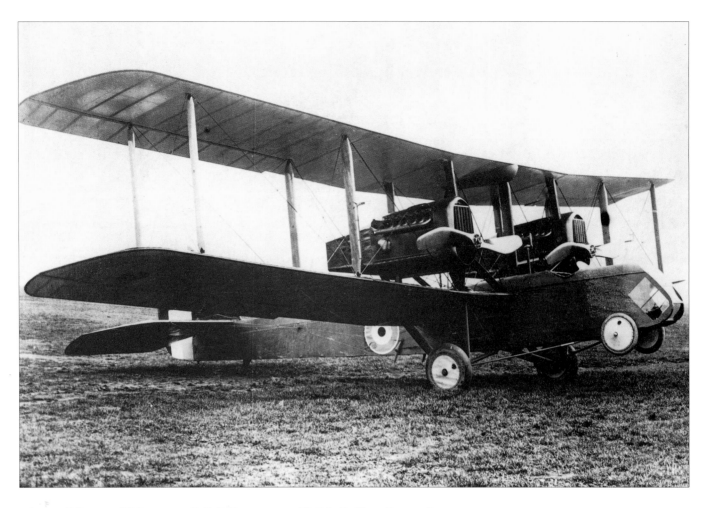

de Havilland/Airco DH10 Amiens

The DH3 produced in 1916 was a large twin-engined pusher configuration biplane heavy bomber. The design was not put into production, and both prototypes were scrapped within a year. The Royal Flying Corps still needed heavy bombers with the range to hit strategic German targets well beyond the front line, and the situation was made more pressing when Germany began its Gotha bomber raids in daylight over London in 1917. Geoffrey de Havilland, realizing that there was not time to start to design a new aircraft from scratch, revisited the DH3 design and used it as the basis for the new bomber aircraft.

The DH10 was similar in layout to the DH3, but was bigger overall and much more robust. The design was swiftly translated into a real aircraft, powered by two BHP 230hp in-line engines in pusher arrangement. The prototype Amiens I (serial C8658) had its maiden flight on March 4, 1918. The trailing edges of the wing had the tell-tale cut-out to allow clearance for the pusher propeller blades. Two other prototypes had the engines installed in the tractor configuration, with the propellers facing forwards. The tractor prototypes were powered by the 360hp Rolls-Royce Eagle VIII (Amiens II, serial C8659, first flight April 20) and the 400hp Liberty 12 (Mk III). In both tractor and pusher configuration, the power plants were positioned between the wings mounted on struts. The fourth prototype had the Liberty engines mounted right on the lower wing, and the performance improved – this version was designated Amiens IIIA or DH10A. Test-flights proved the worth of the design, and the aircraft could fly faster while carrying twice the bomb load of the DH9.

TOP: **The second Amiens prototype. Developed from the earlier DH3, the DH10 arrived just too late to see action during World War I.** ABOVE: **The Amiens IIIA, also known as the DH10A.**

This very capable aircraft was delivered too late for service in World War I, and only eight had been delivered to No.104 Squadron of the then Royal Air Force by the time of the Armistice. Had the war progressed, the aircraft would have been sure to prove its worth in combat.

The original wartime order had been for 1291 aircraft to be built by seven different companies and most were cancelled at the war's end. Some 220 were built, half being the IIIA version engined with either Liberty or Eagle power plants.

Post-war, the Amiens equipped No.216 Squadron in Egypt until it was succeeded by the Vimy in 1923. In Europe the type was well known for its airmail activity, which began in 1919 with No.120 Squadron flying between Hawkinge and Cologne, significantly improving communications with the British Army of the Rhine. In May 1919 an Amiens became the first aircraft to haul mail at night. In June 1921, DH10s pioneered the mail service between Cairo and Baghdad, reportedly using tracks in the desert to assist with navigation.

No.60 Squadron (originally No.97), based at Risalpur on the North West Frontier of India, was the only Royal Air Force unit to use the Amiens bomber in anger. In November 1920 and January 1922 the type was used to carry out bombing raids against rebels in India. The type was replaced there by the DH9A in 1923.

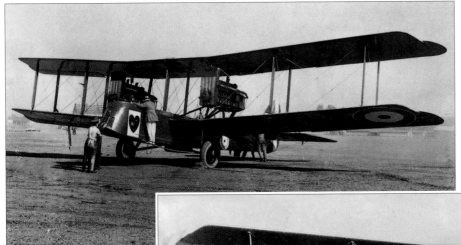

LEFT: **The gentleman peering into the cockpit gives a good idea of the DH10's size.**
BELOW: **Around 220 DH10s were built for Royal Flying Corps/Royal Air Force use, and they served until the early 1920s.** BOTTOM: **A DH10 fitted with tropical radiators, believed to be of No.216 Squadron, based in Egypt.**

de Havilland/Airco DH10 Amiens Mk III

First flight: March 4, 1918
Power: Two 400hp Liberty 12 in-line piston engines
Armament: Two 7.7mm/0.303in machine-guns in nose and rear cockpit; up to 408kg/900lb bomb load
Size: Wingspan – 19.96m/65ft 6in
Length – 12.08m/39ft 7.5in
Height – 4.42m/14ft 6in
Wing area – 77.79m²/837.4sq ft
Weights: Empty – 2535kg/5585lb
Maximum take-off – 4086kg/9000lb
Performance: Maximum speed – 180kph/112mph
Ceiling – 5030m/16,500ft
Endurance – 6 hours
Climb – 4575m/15,000ft in 34 minutes, 30 seconds

de Havilland Mosquito

TOP AND ABOVE: **The Mosquito, the "Wooden Wonder", was one of the first true multi-role aircraft, equally at home in bomber, fighter, nightfighter and photo-reconnaissance roles. The aircraft pictured at the top of the page is a B.Mk V, serial DK338.**

Dubbed the "Wooden Wonder", the Mosquito became the most versatile aircraft to see action during World War II. The Mosquito was a true multi-role combat aircraft which started life in late 1938 as a private venture outline design for a bomber/reconnaissance aircraft that could fly so fast and so high that no defensive armament would be needed.

The wooden construction was chosen because it was very strong when laminated and also kept down the weight, thus providing an excellent high-performance airframe. Another advantage of using wood was that furniture manufacturers could be subcontracted to make the fuselage, wings and tail-plane without disrupting Britain's already overstretched aircraft industry. Wood construction also avoided the use of strategic materials.

Even so, it was only after the start of World War II that Britain's Air Ministry seriously considered the proposal – and then with some caution – but in November 1940 the Mosquito first flew and convinced the sceptics that it was indeed a remarkable aircraft. Priority production was ordered for the bomber version, and meanwhile the photo-reconnaissance and fighter prototypes were prepared.

The first Mosquito prototype was in the Bomber configuration and with its clean airframe and powerful Merlin engines, the aircraft soon proved that it had exceptional

performance and handling characteristics. The Mosquito remained the fastest combat aircraft in the world until 1944. Successful service trials quickly followed and the original March 1940 order for 50 aircraft was subdivided into ten Photo-Reconnaissance Mark Is, ten Bomber Mark VIs and 30 Nightfighters Mark II.

The first Mosquitoes to enter service with the RAF were the Photo-Reconnaissance models in September 1941, and these were used for deep penetration missions over Germany and occupied Europe. During these operations the Mosquito crews found that they were able to outpace all the latest German fighter aircraft.

On November 15, 1941, No.105 Squadron, which was based at RAF Swanton Morley in Norfolk, received its first Mosquito B.IV bomber. However, production of the new aircraft was slow, and it was not until May 1942 that the Squadron flew its first operational sorties to Cologne.

In mid-1943, the B.IX was introduced with increased bomb capacity and the "Oboe" navigational aid for Pathfinder duties. These specialist bombers would lead RAF Bomber Command's Pathfinder Force over enemy territory and lay down target markers. This greatly improved the accuracy of Bomber Command raids and made a significant contribution to the RAF's strategic night-time bomber offensive against the Third Reich.

Fighter-bomber versions were also developed, and the FB.Mk VI became the most widely used of all Mosquito fighters. This version was a day or night intruder, able ultimately to carry up to two 227kg/500lb bombs as well as the usual fighter armament. RAF Coastal Command was quick to see the potential of the type and soon began to use the VI, armed with underwing rockets, as a maritime strike aircraft.

Mosquito crews soon acquired a reputation for the ability to deliver their bomb loads with pinpoint accuracy over both short and long distances. This was ably demonstrated on

February 18, 1944, when 19 Mosquitoes blasted open a German jail at Amiens, which held French resistance fighters. Later, in October 1944, the Gestapo HQ at Aarhus University, Jutland, was bombed with such precision that Danish Resistance leaders were able to escape. *AND A SCHOOL HIT*

In all, 7781 Mosquitoes were built in some 50 variants before production ceased in 1950. The B35 was the ultimate bomber variant of the "Mossie", and it remained in service with RAF Pathfinder units until being replaced by the jet-powered Canberra in 1953. Versions of the Mosquito remained in front-line service with the RAF until December 15, 1955. The Mosquito was a truly magnificent British aircraft.

ABOVE: **The Mosquito had a bomb-carrying capability that staggered crews of heavy bombers. Here, an aircraft of No.692 Squadron based at Gravely in the UK is being loaded with a 1817kg/4000lb bomb for a wartime mission.**
LEFT: **A Mosquito B.Mk IX.** BELOW: **The DZ313 was a B.Mk IV Mosquito powered by Merlin 21 engines.**

---

de Havilland Mosquito B.IV

First flight: November 25, 1940
Power: Two Rolls Royce 1230hp Merlin 21 12-cylinder liquid-cooled in-line piston engines
Armament: 908kg/2000lb bombs
Size: Wingspan – 16.51m/54ft 2in
　　　Length – 12.47m/40ft 10in
　　　Height – 4.66m/15ft 3in
　　　Wing area – 42.18m²/454sq ft
Weights: Empty – 5947kg/13,100lb
　　　Maximum take-off – 10,160kg/22,380lb
Performance: Maximum speed – 612kpg/380mph
　　　Service ceiling – 9455m/31,000ft
　　　Range – 1963km/1220 miles
　　　Climb – 878m/2880ft per minute

Dornier Do17

In 1932 the German Ordnance Department issued development guidelines to a number of leading German aircraft companies for the design and construction of a twin-engine medium bomber with a retractable undercarriage. Dornier designated the project Do17, and covered up the military aspects of the development by describing the aircraft as a fast mail-plane for Deutsche Lufthansa and also a freight carrier for the German State Railways.

On May 17, 1933, the go-ahead was given for the construction of two prototypes, one a high-speed commercial aircraft and the other for "freight" with special equipment – in other words, a bomber. The Do17 bomber prototype first flew in November 1934, and its superior performance caused much concern outside Germany.

At the International Air Show at Dübendorf, Switzerland in 1937, the Do17 MV1 proved to be the leader in its class. It even outpaced a number of European countries' front-line day fighters, including those of France and Czechoslovakia.

The first military examples, the Do17E high-speed bomber and the Do17F long-range reconnaissance aircraft, entered service with the Luftwaffe and saw action during the Spanish Civil War. Both variants were powered by two BMW VI 12-cylinder V-type engines, the Do17F having extra fuel tanks and two bomb bay cameras.

Further development of the Do17 E- and F-types led to the Do17M medium bomber and the Do17P reconnaissance model powered by Bramo 323 radial engines. The definitive variant was the Do17Z, with an extensively glazed cockpit, "beetle" eye, glazed nose and uprated Bramo 323 A-1 engines.

Nicknamed the "Flying Pencil", over 500 Do17Z models were built. Although this aircraft could outpace most contemporary fighters when it entered service with the Luftwaffe in 1938, it soon became obsolete after suffering heavy losses during the Battle of Britain. Nevertheless early in the war, as the Nazis swept through Poland, Norway, the Low Countries and France, the Do17 medium bomber was a key weapon in the German arsenal.

TOP: **The Do17 "Flying Pencil", combat-tested during the Civil War in Spain, was one of the Luftwaffe's most important bomber types.**

ABOVE: **The Do17Z was the main production version, and entered Luftwaffe service in 1938.**

Dornier Do17Z-2

First flight: November 23, 1934 (prototype)
Power: Two BMW Bramo 1000hp 322P Fafnir 9-cylinder radial engines
Armament: One or two 7.92mm/0.31in machine-guns in the windscreen, nose, dorsal and ventral positions; internal bomb load of 1000kg/2205lb
Size: Wingspan – 18m/59ft
Length – 15.8m/51ft 10in
Height – 4.60m/15ft 1in
Wing area – 55m²/592sq ft
Weights: Empty – 5210kg/11,467lb
Maximum take-off – 8590kg/18,906lb
Performance: Maximum speed – 410kph/255mph
Ceiling – 8200m/26,905ft
Range – 1500km/932 miles
Climb – 3000m/9843ft in 8 minutes, 40 seconds

Dornier Do217

TOP AND ABOVE: **The Do217, although mainly inspired by the earlier Do215, was a larger aircraft and differed considerably in many ways. The Do217 could carry the greatest bomb load of all the Luftwaffe bombers of the period.**

At the beginning of 1938 manufacturing specification No.1323 was issued to Dornier for a fast, flexible aircraft that could be used as a medium bomber, long-range reconnaissance or smoke-laying aircraft.

The Do217 was derived from the highly successful Do17/215 series of bombers but was very different to the earlier aircraft. In order to get a quick flying prototype, Dornier modified a Do17-M by adding the Do17Z all-round vision cockpit and increasing the size of the fuselage to enlarge the bomb bay capacity.

The Do217 V-1 prototype first flew in October 1938 but crashed seven days later during single-engine flying tests. The second prototype, Do217 V-2, carried on with the flying-test schedule over the following three months. On February 25, 1939, the third prototype took to the air powered by two Jumo 211-A engines in place of the in-line DB 601s. The Jumo engines were now regarded as essential if the desired performance was to be achieved, and they were fitted to the next two prototypes. However, many other power plants were tried before a final decision was made to use two BMW 801 radials on production models.

The 217 was initially developed as a bomber that carried a greater load than any German bomber of the time. The first production run started at the end of 1940 with the Do217 E-1 medium bomber variant. It was followed by the E-2 and E-3 versions, which differed from the E-1s in their defensive armament and were intended for dive-bombing operations. The Do217 E-4 was identical to the E-2 version apart from a heavy machine-gun in the nose. Other sub-variants included the E-2/R-4 torpedo bomber, the E-2/10 maritime patrol and the E-5, which was capable of carrying radio-controlled air-to-surface missiles.

Dornier Do217 E-2

First flight: October 4, 1938

Power: Two BMW 1580hp 801ML 14-cylinder radial piston engines

Armament: One 20mm/0.78in cannon in lower port side of nose, one 13mm/0.5in machine-gun in dorsal turret and one in ventral step position, one 7.92mm/0.31in machine-gun in nose and one in each side of cockpit; 4000kg/8804lb bomb load

Size: Wingspan – 19m/62ft 4in
Length – 18.20m/ 59ft 8in
Height – 5.03m/16ft 6in
Wing area – 57m²/613.5sq ft

Weights: Empty – 8855kg/19,490lb
Maximum take-off – 16,465kg/36,239lb

Performance: Maximum speed – 515kph/320mph
Ceiling – 9000m/29,530ft
Range – 2800km/1740 miles
Climb – 210m/690ft per minute

Other variants followed, including the three-seat 217J fighter-bomber and nightfighter versions. Both differed from the 217 bomber by having a solid nose in place of the bomber version's "greenhouse" nose for a bomb-aimer.

The J-1 was a fighter-bomber, operational from February 1942, armed with four nose-mounted 7.92mm/0.31in machine-guns and four 20mm/0.78in cannon in addition to dorsal and ventral gun positions, each mounting a pair of 13mm/0.51in guns.

Douglas B-18 Bolo

The twin-engine B-18 Bolo was the first Douglas medium bomber, and was derived from the successful twin-engined DC-2 commercial transport. The B-18 was intended to replace the Martin B-10 in USAAC service. During Air Corps bomber trials at Wright Field in 1935, the B-18 prototype competed with the Martin 146 (an improved B-10) and the four-engine Boeing 299, forerunner of the B-17 Flying Fortress. Surprisingly, only 13 YB-17s were ordered at first as the Army General Staff chose the less costly Bolo and, in January 1936, ordered 133 of the Douglas bombers. Later, 217 more were built as B-18As with a "shark" nose in which the bomb aimer's position was extended forward over the nose gunner's position.

In addition to 133 B-18s, 217 improved B-18As were built, 20 of which were transferred to the Royal Canadian Air Force and designated Digby 1s. During the winter of 1939–40, over 100 B-18As were upgraded to the B-18B standard by installing specialist radio equipment for maritime patrol operations in American and Caribbean waters. These aircraft were used to seek and report the position of German U-boats operating off the US east coast.

The B-18 Bolos were the most numerous US bombers deployed outside the country as the United States entered World War II.

Many B-18s were destroyed by the Japanese at Pearl Harbor on December 7, 1941, and by early 1942 improved aircraft replaced the Bolo as a front-line bomber. Many B-18s were then used as transports or for paratroop training, or modified as B-18Bs for going on anti-submarine duty.

TOP : **The distinctive Douglas tail points to the Bolo's DC-2 origins.**
ABOVE: **This often overlooked bomber was the main type in US use pre-war.** BELOW LEFT: **The bomb aimer's position was over the nose gunner's position, giving the Bolo the so-called "sharknose" look.**

Douglas B-18A Bolo

First flight: April 1935
Power: Two Wright 1000hp R-1820-53 Cyclone 9-cylinder radial engines
Armament: One 7.62mm/0.30in machine-gun in nose, dorsal and ventral positions; up to 2951kg/6500lb of bombs
Size: Wingspan – 27.28m/89ft 6in
Length – 17.63m/57ft 10in
Height – 4.62m/15ft 2in
Wing area – 89.65m²/965sq ft
Weights: Empty – 7409kg/16,321lb
Maximum take-off – 12,563kg/27,673lb
Performance: Maximum speed – 346kph/215mph
Service ceiling – 7,285m/23,900ft
Range – 1931km/1200 miles
Climb – 3048m/10,000ft in 9 minutes, 54 seconds

Douglas SBD-5 Dauntless

The most successful American dive-bomber of World War II had its origins in a 1934 Northrop proposal for a new US Navy dive-bomber based on the Northrop A-17 light attack bomber.

A prototype was ordered and first flew in July 1935, designated XBT-1. After a series of service trials, an order was placed for 54 BT-1 models. The first production batch was fitted with the 825hp Wright R-1535-94 engine. However, the last one off the production line was fitted with a 1000hp R-11820-32 engine and designated XBT-2. Further modifications followed, and after the Northrop Corporation became a division of Douglas in August 1937, the aircraft was redesignated XSBD-1.

It was June 1940 before the US Marine Corps started to receive a batch of 57 Dauntless SBD-1s with their distinctive, large perforated flaps. A few weeks later, the US Navy ordered 82 SBD-2 aircraft with increased fuel capacity, protective cockpit armour and autopilot. After further modifications, the Navy received over 400 SBD-3s during the summer of 1941. By the end of the year, the Dauntless formed the attack element of the US Navy's carrier-based air group in the Pacific. After the Japanese strike on

Pearl Harbor, the SBDs operated from the US aircraft carriers *Lexington* and *Yorktown* during the early months of 1942. They carried out numerous offensive operations against enemy shipping and island shore installations in the build-up to the battle of the Coral Sea. During this battle, the SBDs were joined by the Douglas TBD Devastator torpedo aircraft, and together they attacked and sank the Japanese light carrier *Shoho* and damaged the fleet carrier *Shokaku*. This was followed in June 1942 by the Battle of Midway, where SBDs from the carriers *Enterprise*, *Hornet* and *Yorktown* had a major success by sinking the Japanese carriers *Akagi*, *Kaga* and *Soryu*, and damaging the *Hiryu* so badly that it had to be scuttled. By the end of the battle, Japan had lost most of its capital ships in the Pacific.

In October 1942 the SBD-4 made its appearance fitted with radar and radio navigation equipment. This was followed in large quantities by the SBD-5, which had a more powerful 1200hp engine. One SBD-5 was fitted with a 1350hp R-1820-66 engine and used as a prototype for the SBD-6. This was the last Dauntless variant to be produced, and it appeared in early 1944.

Douglas SBD-5 Dauntless

First flight: July 1935

Power: One Wright 1200hp R-1820-60 Cyclone 9-cylinder radial engine

Armament: Two 12.7mm/0.5in fixed forward-firing machine-guns in upper part of the forward fuselage, two trainable 7.62mm/0.3in machine-guns in rear cockpit; external bomb or depth charge load of 1021kg/2250lb

Size: Wingspan – 12.66m/41ft 6in
Length – 10.09m/33ft 1in
Height – 4.14m/13ft 7in
Wing area – 30.19m²/325sq ft

Weights: Empty – 2963kg/6521lb
Maximum take-off – 4858kg/10,700lb

Performance: Maximum speed – 410kph/255mph
Ceiling – 7786m/25,530ft
Range – 2519km/1565 miles
Climb – 457m/1500ft per minute

ABOVE: **The Dauntless inflicted massive damage on enemy ships in the Pacific war, serving the US Navy and Marine Corps throughout World War II.**
BELOW: **This photograph shows the SBD's trademark perforated flaps.**

Douglas A-20 Boston/Havoc

The story of the Douglas DB-7 family of combat aircraft is complicated by the variety of names by which the numerous bomber, nightfighter and intruder versions were known. The complex DB-7/A-20/Havoc/Boston story began with Douglas submitting their DB-7 to meet a 1938 US Army specification for an attack aircraft. The result was an advanced and complex design which incorporated the novel nosewheel undercarriage arrangement for better pilot visibility on the ground. The aircraft also featured a highly unusual emergency second control column for the rear gunner's use in the event of the pilot being incapacitated.

France placed an order for 100 DB-7 models in February 1940, and some of these aircraft did see service with the French Armée de l'Air. Some of these aircraft flew to Britain to fight on against the Nazis, while some remained to be used by the Vichy Air Force. However, the principal early user of the Douglas design in Europe was the Royal Air Force, with whom the Havoc nightfighter/intruder version entered service in April 1941. A three-seat intruder version carried a 908kg/2000lb bomb load for use against targets in France, and was certainly a nuisance to the enemy under cover of darkness.

The first of the DB-7 series to serve as an RAF bomber was the Boston III variant (USAAF A-20C). This daylight bombing role was the one for which the aircraft was first designed. The first IIIs arrived in the UK from the USA in the summer of 1941 and soon replaced the Blenheims of No.2 Group, carrying out anti-shipping missions as well as bombing raids. A total of 781 Boston IIIs were delivered to the RAF, and the first to enter service did so with No.88 Squadron at Swanton Morley in October 1941. They saw action for the first time on February 12, 1942, and went on to fly many missions against targets in France, Belgium and the Netherlands, frequently flying

TOP: **The solid-nosed A-20G was the most numerous and main operational variant of the series serving in Europe, the Mediterranean and the Pacific, mainly in the low-level attack role.** ABOVE: **An RAF Boston III – note the forward gun blister fairing housing just above the nosewheel, containing the 7.7mm/0.303in machine-guns.**

perilously low to avoid enemy defences. They also took part in attacks on the German warships *Scharnhorst*, *Prinz Eugen* and *Gneisenau*, when they took part in the famous channel dash. The IIIs also served with the RAF in Italy, Tunisia and Algeria. On July 4, 1942, RAF Bostons attacked airfields in Holland – this raid was unusual because six of the aircraft involved were flown by crews of the US Eighth Air Force, giving the Mighty Eighth its first taste of battle in Europe. As more heavy bombers entered RAF service, the Bostons were restricted to tactical operations.

As part of the D-Day operations, British-based Bostons of the Second Tactical Air Force generated smoke screens over the invasion beaches. 1944 also saw the introduction of the Boston IV (the A-20G in USAAF service) and the Boston V (USAAF A-20H) distinguished from earlier versions by its power-operated gun turret. This version served with the RAF in the Second Tactical Air Force until the end of war in Europe in close co-operation with advancing ground troops. In USAAF service, the A-20G served with the Ninth Air Force in Europe, the Twelfth in the Mediterranean and in the Pacific with the Fifth Air Force. Around half of all the A-20G models produced were supplied to the Soviet Union. Total production of all versions was 7478 aircraft.

RIGHT: **An early A-20A Havoc.** BELOW: **BD121 was built as a Boston I, then converted to Havoc intruder standard. Note the flame damper exhausts and matt black paint for maximum concealment at night.**

ABOVE: **USAAF Havocs first saw action when they came under attack during the Japanese strike at Pearl Harbor in December 1941.**

Douglas Boston IV/A-20G

First flight: October 26, 1938 (Douglas 7B prototype)

Power: Two Wright 1700hp R-2600-23 14-cylinder radial engines

Armament: Six 12.7/0.50in machine-guns in the nose, two in dorsal position and one in ventral position; bomb load of 1816kg/4000lb

Size: Wingspan – 18.69m/61ft 4in
Length – 14.63m/47ft 11in
Height – 5.36m/17ft 7in
Wing area – 43.11m²/464sq ft

Weights: Empty – 7256kg/15,984lb
Maximum take-off – 12,348kg/27,200lb

Performance: Maximum speed – 546kph/339mph
Service ceiling – 7869m/25,800ft
Range – 3380km/2100 miles
Climb – 3048m/10,000ft in 7 minutes, 6 seconds

Douglas A-26/B-26 Invader

TOP: **The A-26 was the fastest bomber the USA had in its World War II inventory.**
ABOVE: **The Invader served in three major conflicts of the 20th century, and had three designations in its service life.**

There are some combat aircraft that have served in two major wars, but few have served in three conflicts spread over more than two decades. The Invader did just that in World War II, Korea and Vietnam.

In 1940, before it could get detailed information on combat experiences in Europe, the USAAF issued a requirement for an attack aircraft to be built in three different prototype forms – attack, nightfighter and bomber. After the prototypes had flown (the XA-26 bomber version was first to fly, on July 10, 1942) it was the attack version that was selected first for production under the designation A-26B. Armed with six machine-guns in the solid nose and up to 14 more in remotely controlled turrets or underwing gunpacks, the heavily-armed Invader could also carry up to 1816kg/4000lb of bombs. This was a formidable and fast ground-attack aircraft – it was in fact the fastest American bomber of World War II.

The A-26B made its debut in the European theatre with the US Ninth Air Force in November 1944. The destructive power of the aircraft was used to maximum effect by bombing, ground strafing and launching rocket attacks in advance of the Allied ground forces as they fought their way through Europe. The aircraft was also used for dropping allied agents into enemy territory. Invaders had entered service in the Pacific at the same time.

1945 saw the entry of the A-26C into front-line service, and this version differed by having only two guns in a glazed nose and room for a bomb-aimer's position. This version saw little use before the end of the war, by which time 1091 examples had been built compared to 1355 B-models.

In the immediate post-war period, some Invaders were converted for use as target tugs for the US Navy, designated JD-1 (later the UB-26J). In 1948, USAF A-26 aircraft were redesignated B-26, not to be confused with the unrelated Martin B-26 Marauder withdrawn from USAF service in 1948.

LEFT: *My Baby*, B-26B, pictured in Korea in 1950. Note the nose, bristling with guns. BELOW: **Equally potent armament can be seen in the nose of this French Air Force Invader pictured in Indo-China, March 1951.**

In 1950, USAF Invaders took part in the first (and three years later the last) combat mission of the Korean War, where over 450 Invaders – both B-26B and B-26C models saw extensive USAF service, principally as night-intruders. Meanwhile, France also used them in Indo-China against the Viet Minh.

As tensions grew in Vietnam, Invaders were deployed to South Vietnam in 1962 and although they were painted in South Vietnamese markings, the aircraft flew into combat with US crews on board. After an aircraft disintegrated in mid-air due to wing stress problems, the B-26 was withdrawn from Vietnam. However, the USAF was keen to not lose the capability of the B-26 and invited On Mark Engineering, a company who had already carried out civilian conversions of the B-26, to produce a very heavily armed, dedicated counter-insurgency (COIN) version for use in South-east Asia. Low-hour airframes were extensively converted, essentially producing 40 brand new aircraft, the B-26K. These rebuilt aircraft saw extensive use in Vietnam in the ground-attack and interdiction roles until 1970, often flown by men younger than the aircraft itself.

The Invader's identity crisis was further complicated in 1966, when the B-26K was redesignated the A-26A for political reasons. The USAF wanted to base B-26K Invaders in Thailand, but the Thai government did not want bombers operating from their country. The B-26K was simply redesignated the A-26A, an attack aircraft, which was acceptable to the Thai government.

Some air forces still had Invaders as front-line aircraft into the late 1970s. When the fast Invader was declared surplus, many were well-used for civilian purposes, from executive transports to firebombers and crop-sprayers.

ABOVE: **The A/B-26 Invader family of aircraft served extensively around the world, with some still on active duty into the 1970s.**

Douglas B-26B Invader

First flight: July 10, 1942
Power: Two Pratt & Whitney 2000hp R-2800-27 18-cylinder radial piston engines
Armament: Ten 12.7mm/0.50in machine-guns mounted in nose, dorsal and ventral turrets; bomb load of 1816kg/4,000lb
Size: Wingspan – 21.34m/70ft
Length – 15.42m/50ft
Height – 5.64m/18ft 6in
Wing area – 50.17m²/540sq ft
Weights: Empty – 10,373kg/22,850lb
Maximum take-off – 15,890kg/35,000lb
Performance: Maximum speed – 571kph/355mph
Service ceiling – 6740m/22,100ft
Range – 2253km/1400 miles
Climb – 610m/2000ft per minute

Fairey Swordfish

The Swordfish holds a special place in aviation history because it is one of the few combat aircraft to be operational at both the start and end of World War II. This remarkable aircraft was also the last British military biplane in front-line service, and had the distinction of serving longer than the aircraft intended to replace it in Fleet Air Arm service. The "Stringbag" was developed from an earlier failed Fairey design and first flew in April 1934, designated TSR (torpedo spotter reconnaissance).

After successful service trials, a contract to supply 86 Swordfish Mk Is to the Royal Navy's Fleet Air Arm was signed. The Swordfish entered service with No.825 Squadron in July 1936, and over the next three years a further 600 aircraft were delivered, equipping 13 Fleet Air Arm squadrons. During World War II another 12 squadrons were formed.

The wartime exploits of this deceptively frail-looking aircraft are legendary. Its first major action was against the Italian naval base at Taranto on November 11, 1940. HMS *Illustrious* launched 21 Swordfish of Nos.815 and 819 Squadrons to make a night attack on the Italian fleet. During the raid the Swordfish destroyed three battleships, two destroyers, a cruiser and other smaller ships for the loss of only two of the attacking aircraft. The attack crippled the Italian fleet and eliminated the opportunity for Italian warships to bolster German naval strength in the Mediterranean.

Other notable actions include the crippling of the German battleship *Bismarck* in May 1941. Swordfish from the Royal Navy carriers HMS *Victorious* and HMS *Ark Royal* were involved in the search for the German battleship. The first Swordfish attack, led by Lieutenant Commander Esmonde,

LEFT: **Each of these D-Day period Swordfish bears stripes on both sets of wings and the fuselage, giving the aircraft a zebra-like appearance. There were few Allied biplanes in the front line at the time of D-Day.**
BELOW: **The "Stringbag" was involved in many notable World War II actions, the most famous of which is probably the Swordfish attack on the Italian fleet at Taranto.**

was launched from *Victorious* but none of the torpedoes from the nine aircraft caused serious damage. During the second attack, delivered by 20 Swordfish from the *Ark Royal*, a torpedo severely damaged *Bismarck's* rudder, greatly limiting the ship's manoeuverability. The pursuing British task force was then able to catch and finally sink *Bismarck* with naval gunfire.

Then in February 1942, crews of No.825 Squadron carried out a gallant attack against the *Scharnhorst*, *Gneisenau* and *Prinz Eugen*, during which all six aircraft were shot down. Only five of the 18 crew members survived. For his bravery and leadership under fire, Lieutenant Commander Esmonde, veteran of the *Bismarck* mission and leader of the attack, was posthumously awarded the Victoria Cross.

While the Mk I was an all-metal, fabric-covered aircraft, the Mk II Swordfish which entered service in 1943 had metal-clad lower wings to enable the aircraft to fire rocket projectiles.

Later the same year, ASV (air-to-surface-vessel) radar was installed between the aircraft's fixed undercarriage legs on Mk IIIs, while the Mk IV had an enclosed cockpit.

During the desperate Battle of the Atlantic, there were simply not enough aircraft carriers to escort Allied convoys across the ocean. As a stopgap measure to provide some protection for the convoys, Britain converted grain ships and oil tankers to become MAC ships (Merchant Aircraft Carriers). Grain ships, fitted with a 122m/400ft flight deck, a below-deck hangar and lift, operated four Swordfish. The tankers had a 140m/460ft flight deck but no hangar in which to accommodate their three Swordfish – the MAC Swordfish suffered considerable wear and tear.

From 1940 all development and production of the Swordfish passed from Fairey to the Blackburn Aircraft Company, which built 1699 of the 2391 aircraft produced. The last RN Swordfish squadron disbanded in May 1945.

ABOVE: **The Swordfish outlasted the aircraft intended to replace it in Fleet Air Arm service, the Albacore.** LEFT: **An excellent air-to-air study of Swordfish, complete with 45cm/18in torpedo. Note the bomb shackles beneath the wing.** BELOW: **Thirteen Fleet Air Arm squadrons were equipped with the "Stringbag" when war broke out.**

Fairey Swordfish Mk I

First flight: April 17, 1934
Power: One Bristol 690hp Pegasus IIIM3 9-cylinder air-cooled radial engine
Armament: One fixed 7.7mm/0.303in Browning machine-gun in the nose and one flexible 7.7mm/0.303in Vickers or Lewis machine gun in the rear cockpit; one 45cm/18in 731kg/1610lb torpedo or one 681kg/1500lb mine or bombs
Size: Wingspan – 13.87m/45ft 6in
  Length – 10.87m/35ft 8in
  Height – 3.76m/12ft 4in
  Wing area – 56.39m²/607sq ft
Weights: Empty – 2134kg/4700lb
  Maximum take-off – 3409kg/7510lb
Performance: Maximum speed – 222kph/138mph
  Service ceiling – 5029m/16,500ft
  Range – 1658km/1030 miles unloaded
  Climb – 3050m/10,000ft in 15 minutes, 2 seconds

Fairey Battle

The Fairey Battle which first flew on March 10, 1936 was initially known as the Fairey Day Bomber. It had its origins in a 1932 Air Ministry specification, and was a single-engine light bomber with a crew of three, designed to replace the Hind and Hart biplanes in Royal Air Force service. This low-wing stressed-skin monoplane was the epitome of modern aircraft design in the mid-1930s, replacing fabric-covered biplanes and boasting a retractable undercarriage, variable-pitch propellers and a cockpit canopy. Impressively, it could carry twice the bomb load over the twice the distance of the aircraft it was to replace. Nevertheless when it went to war, it was an aircraft out of time and proved to be under-powered and inadequately armed for modern air combat.

The famous Merlin engine is forever linked to the Battle of Britain duo, the Spitfire and Hurricane, but the Fairey Battle was the first aircraft to be fitted with the new high-performance Rolls-Royce engine. The five main marks of the Battle (I–V) were designated thus depending which version of the Merlin engine, I to V, was used for power.

Battles entered RAF service in May 1937 and ultimately equipped 15 RAF bomber squadrons. By the time Britain entered World War II in September 1939, over 1000 aircraft were in service with the RAF.

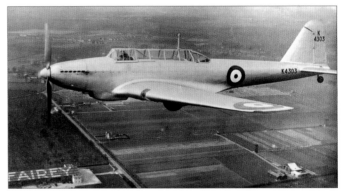

TOP: **Three Stockport-built Fairey Battle Is of No.218 Squadron, Royal Air Force. The Battle could carry a much greater bomb load than those aircraft that it replaced, but it was underpowered.** ABOVE: **K4303, the Battle prototype, pictured over a Fairey airfield. Note that this aircraft has a propeller spinner fitted, but service aircraft did not have this refinement.**

When Britain sent the Advanced Air Striking Force to France in September 1939, ten squadrons of Battles were the main offensive component. On September 20, 1939, a Battle of No.88 Squadron claimed the first German aircraft downed on the "western front". However, the Battle was no match for nimble monoplane fighters, and was simply no longer suited to unescorted daylight missions. On September 30, 1939, when four out of five Battles of No.150 Squadron were shot down by Bf109s, unescorted missions ceased.

Fairey Battle Mk I

First flight: March 10, 1936
Power: One Rolls-Royce 1030hp Merlin
12-cylinder piston engine
Armament: One 7.7mm/0.303in machine-gun in
leading edge of starboard wing and one in rear
cockpit; bomb load of 454kg/1000lb
Size: Wingspan – 16.45m/54ft
Length – 12.90m/42ft 4in
Height – 4.57m/15ft
Wing area – 39.2m²/422sq ft
Weights: Empty – 3018kg/6647lb
Maximum take-off – 4899kg/10,792lb
Performance: Maximum speed – 414kph/257mph
Service ceiling – 7930m/26,000ft
Range – 1609km/1000 miles
Climb – 280m/920ft per minute

TOP: **Over 1000 Battles were in RAF service when war broke out, and the type
was sent into action early in the conflict. All was well until the Battle faced the
best Luftwaffe fighters on the day and suffered heavy losses. By 1941 most
were being used for training.** ABOVE: **On one operation in May 1940, 40 out of
71 aircraft were lost on a daylight raid against enemy targets.** RIGHT: **The Fairey
P4/34, inspired by the Battle and resembling a scaled-down version of it, began
as a light bomber prototype. The aircraft was developed into a two-seat fighter
for the Royal Navy, the Fulmar.**

When the Blitzkrieg reached France in May 1940, these
Battles were thrown into the thick of the fighting in desperation,
doing battle with the most modern German fighters, and
they suffered terrible losses. On May 10, operating at heights
of around 76m/250ft, the Battles attacked German ground
forces with delayed-fuse bombs and suffered high losses from
ground fire – 13 of 32 aircraft were lost. On May 14, a force
of 71 Battles was sent to bomb German bridges at Sedan
and only 31 aircraft returned to their bases.

By the end of June 1940, all Battles were recalled to Britain
but the type continued to be used for attacks against enemy-
held Channel ports as well as the crucial raids against the
German invasion barges in the Channel ports in September 1940.

Once removed from front-line duties, Battles were used as
training aircraft, target-tugs and for teaching air gunnery. A
dedicated two-cockpit Battle Trainer, a truly strange-looking
aircraft, helped many British and Commonwealth pilots earn
their wings.

Eight hundred were shipped to Canada and 400 to Australia
for these purposes under the Empire Air Training Scheme
(EATS). Battles remained in Royal Australian Air Force use
until 1949.

Battles were also exported to Turkey (29), South Africa
(190 plus) who used them in action in East Africa, and
Belgium where 18 were built under licence by Avions Fairey.
These Belgian Battles suffered the same fate at their RAF
counterparts as they bravely fought against much more
modern aircraft.

Fairey Barracuda

The Fairey Aviation Company's response to Specification S.24/37 for a Fairey Albacore replacement was the three-seat Barracuda, which had its maiden flight on December 7, 1940. Testing highlighted some shortcomings that were resolved in the second prototype, but this did not fly until June 1941. Britain's aviation industry was focusing on the production of fighters and bombers at the time, and the new torpedo bomber just had to wait. Service trials were therefore not complete until February 1942, after which the more powerful Merlin 32 was fitted. The new engine was required to cope with the increasing weight of the Barracuda due to a beefing-up of the structure and additional equipment to be carried. The re-engined Barracuda became the Mark II, the main production variant of the type. The Mark IIs began to enter service in early 1943, the first 12 Mark IIs going to No.827 Squadron, then re-forming at Stretton. By May 1943, many squadrons of the Fleet Air Arm became fully equipped with Barracuda Mk IIs and then joined carriers of the home and Far Eastern fleets. The Barracuda has a number of claims to fame – it was the first British carrier-based monoplane of all-metal construction to enter service with the Fleet Air Arm, as well as being the first monoplane torpedo bomber. A total of 1688 Barracuda Mk IIs were built by Fairey, as well as Westland, Blackburn and Boulton Paul.

The Barracuda Mark III (912 examples built by Fairey and Boulton Paul) was developed to carry air-to-surface-vessel radar in a radome blister under the rear fuselage, and first flew

TOP: **A fine air-to-air study of a Fairey (Heaton Chapel-built) Barracuda Mk I.** ABOVE: **A great visual explanation of the below-deck space saving that can be achieved by having naval aircraft with folding wings.**

in 1943. The radar enabled the Barracuda to track its prey much more effectively. In European waters, Mark IIIs equipped with ASV radar flew anti-submarine patrols from small escort carriers, using rocket-assisted take-off to get clear of the short decks.

In April 1944, the carriers *Victorious* and *Furious* sent 42 Barracudas to carry out a dive-bombing attack on the German pocket battleship *Tirpitz*, then at anchor in Kaa Fjord, Norway.

The Barracudas were part of Operation Tungsten, the aim of which was the destruction of the enemy ship. The Barracudas had practised long and hard for the operation, and attacked in a steep dive despite heavy defensive flak. They scored 15 direct hits with armour-piercing bombs for the loss of only two aircraft. *Tirpitz* was so damaged in the raid that it was out of action for three months, and the Navy was able to channel its resources elsewhere, at least for a time.

Nos.810 and 847 Squadrons, Fleet Air Arm, which were embarked on HMS *Illustrious*, introduced the Barracuda to the Pacific theatre of operations in April 1944, when they supported the US Navy in a dive-bombing attack on the Japanese installations on Sumatra.

In all, 17 operational Fleet Air Arm squadrons were equipped with Barracudas during World War II. Wartime production of the Fairey Barracuda totalled 2541 aircraft. In 1945, production started on the more powerful Mk V, later designated the TF.5, but only 30 models of this variant were built and were used as trainers during the post-war period.

No fewer than 2572 Barracudas of all marks were delivered to the FAA. Barracudas were also operated by the French and Dutch Fleet Air Arms.

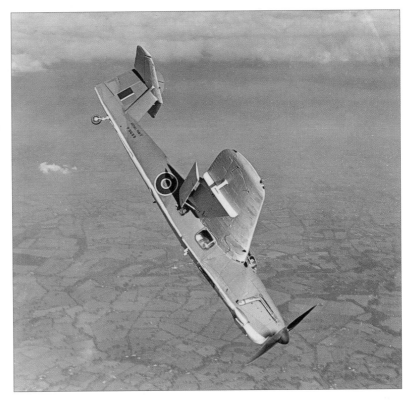

ABOVE RIGHT: **The Barracuda was instrumental in severely damaging the *Tirpitz* during April 1944.** RIGHT: **The ultimate Barracuda, the Mk V appeared too late for war use, and was destined for post-war training instead.** BELOW: **With the carrier deck crew watching intently, a Fleet Air Arm Barracuda prepares to catch the arrestor wire with its hook.**

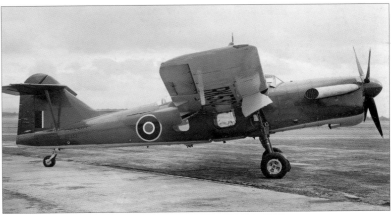

Fairey Barracuda Mk II

First flight: December 7, 1940

Power: One Rolls-Royce 1640hp Merlin 32 V-12 piston engine

Armament: Two 7.7mm/0.303in Browning machine-guns in rear cockpit; one 735kg/1620lb torpedo or one 454kg/1000lb bomb beneath fuselage, or four 204kg/450lb or six 113kg/250lb bombs, depth charges or mines under wings

Size: Wingspan – 14.99m/49ft 2in
Length – 12.12m/39ft 9in
Height – 4.60m/15ft 1in
Wing area – 34.09m²/367sq ft

Weights: Empty – 4245kg/9350lb
Maximum take-off – 6401kg/14,100lb

Performance: Maximum speed – 367kph/228mph
Ceiling – 5060m/16,600ft
Range – 1851km/1150 miles
Climb – 1524m/5000ft in 6 minutes

Focke-Wulf Fw200

The Fw200 Condor maritime reconnaissance bomber aircraft had its origins in a Deutsche Lufthansa airliner. The Fw200 was a low-wing, all-metal, four-engine monoplane with fully retractable undercarriage which could carry 26 passengers. The aircraft was a headline-grabber in 1937, and set numerous records pre-war for non-stop flights from Germany to New York and Tokyo. Finland, Denmark and Brazil ordered the airliner but the military capabilities of the large aircraft were not lost on the Japanese who were the first to ask for a military long-range maritime-reconnaissance version. This development prototype, known as the Fw200V-10, had a large below-floor cabin grafted on to the underside of the fuselage, which carried the aircraft's bomb load as well as defensive machine-guns. The aircraft's obvious applications came to the attention of the Luftwaffe, who then requested a prototype of their own, the Fw200C, for evaluation. As World War II broke out and the Luftwaffe needed a long-range maritime-patrol and attack aircraft, their prototype version was pressed into production.

TOP AND ABOVE: **The military potential of the Fw200 was apparently first considered by the Japanese. Had Germany developed the Condor into a heavy bomber early in the war and produced large numbers, this could have been a major threat to Britain. However, the Luftwaffe were more concerned with tactical aircraft than "heavies".**

The first Luftwaffe unit to receive the Condor (and its main operator for the war) was Kampfgeschwader (KG) 40 in April 1940. With a crew of five (pilot, co-pilot and three gunners), the Condor flew its first mission against British shipping on April 8, 1940, while operating from Denmark. Two months later, the unit was transferred to France, from where it operated until

ABOVE: **Operating from France, and not in huge numbers, the Fw200s caused great losses to British shipping.** BELOW RIGHT: **The Condor could also act as an airborne command post, directing U-boats towards allied shipping.**

Focke-Wulf Fw200C-3 Condor

First flight: July 27, 1937 (civil model)

Power: Four BMW-Bramo 1200hp 323R-2 Fafnir 9-cylinder radial engines

Armament: One 7.92mm/0.31in gun in forward dorsal turret, one 13mm/0.5in gun in rear dorsal position, two 13mm/0.5in guns in beak positions, one 20mm/0.78in gun in forward position of ventral gondola and one 7.92mm/0.31in gun in aft ventral position; maximum bomb load of 2100kg/4622lb

Size: Wingspan – 32.85m/107ft 9in

Length – 23.45m/76ft 11in

Height – 6.30m/20ft 8in

Wing area – 119.85m²/1290sq ft

Weights: Empty – 17,005kg/37,428lb

Maximum take-off – 24,520kg/53,968lb

Performance: Maximum speed – 360kph/224mph

Service ceiling – 6000m/19,685ft

Range – 3560km/2212 miles

Climb – 200m/656ft per minute

late 1944. By the end of September 1940, the Condors had sunk 91,440 tonnes/90,000 tons of Allied shipping, and Churchill soon referred to these aircraft as "the scourge of the Atlantic".

By December 1940, 36 aircraft were operational, and during 1941, 58 Mk C-2s were built, fitted with bomb racks in the outboard engine nacelle and beneath the wing. Structural problems with the Condor's rear fuselage manifested themselves early in the aircraft's career, with a number simply breaking their backs on landing. An improved, strengthened version with much more powerful engines, the Fw200C-3, was being built by mid-1941.

As the Condor became more numerous and crews learned the art of maritime surveillance and attack, the aircraft became a major threat to Allied shipping – 328,185 tonnes/323,016 tons (116 ships) were sunk during April 1941 alone. The radius of operation could be extended even further as long-range fuel tanks would increase endurance from the normal 9 hours, 45 minutes to 18 hours.

The final version of the Condor to see service was the Fw200C-6 armed with a Henschel Hs293B air-to-surface missile beneath each wing. The total wartime Fw200 production was 252 aircraft.

Despite the relatively small numbers, the Condor fleet proved to be a major concern for the Allies – not only could the Condor attack a ship on its own, it could also direct U-boats towards convoys. The Condor's reign ended in late 1944 as the Allies overran Luftwaffe bases in France. Surviving Fw200s earned their keep as transports. The chief of the Gestapo, Heinrich Himmler, had a Condor as his personal transport. Well armoured, the VIP transport boasted a large leather chair, as well as a personal escape hatch for the occupant.

ABOVE: **The "scourge of the Atlantic", as Churchill once described the Condor fleet, was only stopped when the Allies seized their French bases after D-Day.**

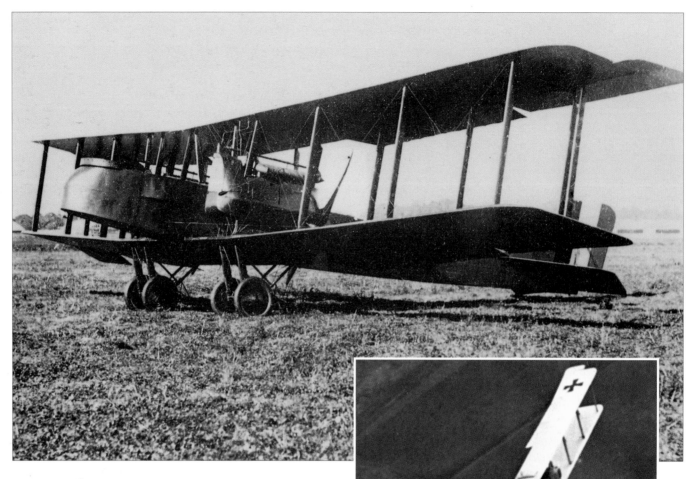

Gotha bombers

As a result of unexpected and seemingly unstoppable bombing raids by German bombers over London in 1917–18, for some civilians the word "Gotha" became synonymous with terror. Development of the series of bombers began in 1915 with the Gotha G.II, which entered service on the Eastern Front in the autumn of 1916. Repeated engine failures led to its withdrawal and the appearance of the G.III with two machine-guns and the more reliable Mercedes D IVa engine. By December 1916, 14 were in front-line service, each able to carry a 400kg/880lb bomb load.

The Germans had been keen to carry out sustained bombing raids over London, and were able to do this with their Zeppelin airships until British defences got the measure of their hydrogen-filled adversaries. A heavier-than-air alternative was needed, and so the Gotha G.IV was conceived. Some sources claim the aircraft's development was greatly helped by the capture of a brand new Handley Page O/400 in early 1917.

The G.IV was made of wood and steel, and covered with plywood and fabric. An unusual feature was the "firing tunnel" tested on some G.IIIs, which enabled the gunner to fire down "through" the floor to defend the aircraft's rear most effectively by eliminating the blind-spot favoured by stalking fighter aircraft. Power was provided by two Mercedes D.IVa in-line piston engines mounted between the wings and driving pusher

TOP AND ABOVE: **The Gotha was one of the first bombers able to take the war far beyond the front line and right to the heart of the enemy's homeland. Gotha raids on London in 1917–18 caused panic and damage to morale.**

propellers. To give clearance to the spinning wooden prop blades behind the wings, the trailing edge of the upper wing had a large section removed. When testing proved the soundness of the aircraft's design, production began by Gotha, LVG and Siemens-Schuckert.

When formations of Gothas headed to hostile territory they were able to cover each other with defensive fire from their two 7.92mm/0.31in Parabellum machine-guns, something lone Zeppelin raiders lacked on their 51 bombing raids over Britain in World War I. The G.IV was able to carry up to 500kg/1100lb of bombs in cradles beneath the wing, and two primitive rectangular bomb bays between the pilot and the rear crewman contained up to six bombs, each stacked one on the other so that as the lowest bomb was released, all of the rest followed.

The first large Gotha raid on Britain took place on May 25, 1917, when 21 Gothas bombed Folkestone in Kent, killing almost 100 civilians. Within three weeks, the first daylight raid on London was carried out by a formation of 14 Gothas. The raids continued each day, with the Gothas flying at heights of 3050–4880m/10,000–16,000ft up the Thames Estuary, too high for the defenders to reach them. However, to achieve these altitudes the Gothas had to reduce their bomb load, which was at its maximum on night raids when lower altitudes were safer. The raids against southern England were launched mainly from the German bases St Denis Westrem and Gontrode in Belgium. These airfields were frequently attacked by British bombers trying to remove the threat to the homeland at source. The Gotha raids were costly in lives but were also damaging financially and psychologically for the civilians who experienced the raids. By early 1918, the raiders were suffering heavy losses to the guns of the fast-climbing British S.E.5a and Sopwith Camel defending fighters, even at night.

August 1917 had seen the introduction of the G.V, an improved version of the IV which featured more aerodynamic engine nacelles to reduce drag. The final versions in service were the G.Va, with a biplane tail assembly and a shorter nose, and the G.Vb which had a nose wheel for improved landing safety on night operations.

The 22 Gotha raids on Britain had seen these early bombers drop a remarkable total of 84.3 tonnes/83 tons of bombs on the country.

TOP RIGHT: **A Gotha V, featuring more streamlined engine nacelles.**
RIGHT: **The Gotha G.VII was produced as a long-range reconnaissance aircraft, with the nosegun position deleted and the engines repositioned closer to the fuselage and in a puller configuration.** BELOW: **Formations of Gothas were early users of the box formation best associated with the Eighth Air Force bombers of World War II. The Gothas positioned themselves to provide mutual cover against enemy aircraft.**

Gotha G.V

First flight: Early 1917
Power: Two Mercedes 260hp D IVa in-line piston engines
Armament: Two 7.92mm/0.31in machine-guns on mounts in nose and dorsal positions; up to 500kg/1100lb bomb load
Size: Wingspan – 23.7m/77ft 9in
Length – 11.86m/38ft 11in
Height – 4.3m/14ft 1.25in
Wing area – 89.5m²/963.4sq ft
Weights: Empty – 2740kg/6030lb
Maximum take-off – 3975kg/8748lb
Performance: Maximum speed – 140kph/87mph
Ceiling – 6500m/21,325ft
Range – 500km/311 miles
Climb – 3000m/9840ft in 28 minutes

Grumman Avenger

Grumman's large single-engine torpedo bomber certainly lived up to the name "Avenger" given to it on the day that Japan attacked Pearl Harbor. Procured in great quantities, the type saw action with Allied air arms in virtually all theatres of operation in World War II. Of the 9836 aircraft produced, 2290 were built by Grumman (and designated TBF) while the remaining TBM models were manufactured by the General Motors Eastern Division.

The Avenger was designed in just five weeks, and was first flown on August 1, 1941. With a three-man crew, the aircraft featured an internal weapons bay, gun turret and a rear defensive gun position. A door on the right-side rear of the wing allowed access into the rear fuselage, which was packed with equipment, flares, parachutes and ammunition. At the lower level, the bombardier was provided with a folding seat from which he could either man the lower rear machine-gun, or face forward and aim the aircraft for medium-altitude level bombing. The pilot sat in a roomy and comfortable cockpit above the leading edge, and enjoyed an excellent view.

Only one aircraft returned from the six that made the Avenger's combat debut at the Battle of Midway in June 1942. Despite this poor start, the Avenger went on to become one of the great naval combat aircraft of World War II, being involved in the destruction of more than 60 Japanese warships. It was the first US single-engined aircraft able to

TOP AND ABOVE: **The Grumman Avenger and Tarpon, one and the same. The Royal Navy quickly dropped the Tarpon name and standardized on the original US one. The excellent Avenger was designed in just five weeks.**

carry the hard-hitting 560mm/22in torpedo (as well as depth charges, rockets and bombs) and was also the first to boast a power-operated gun turret. Torpedoes launched by US Navy Avengers were largely responsible for the sinking of the large Japanese battleships *Yamato* and *Musashi*.

The Royal Navy received 402 Avengers (TBF-1Bs) under the Anglo-American Lend-Lease arrangement with the first squadron, No.832 Squadron (on board HMS *Victorious*), being equipped in early 1943. Although originally designated Tarpon Mk I for British service, they were later redesignated Avenger Mk I. Around 330 TBM-1s were also supplied to the Royal Navy, and designated Avenger Mk II.

Delivery of the TBM-3 began in April 1944, with the Royal Navy receiving the 222 TBM-3 aircraft designated Avenger Mk III by the British. Torpedo bomber versions remained in

ABOVE AND RIGHT: **Although the Avenger had a shaky combat debut during the Battle of Midway, it was soon shown to be among the best naval fighting aircraft ever produced. Avengers lived up to their name and were solely or partly responsible for the destruction of over 60 Japanese naval targets.**

RN service until 1947 and then, in 1953, the Royal Navy began acquiring anti-submarine versions designated the Avenger AS Mk IV or AS Mk V. The Avenger finally retired from the Royal Navy in 1962.

In 1951, the Royal Canadian Navy anti-submarine units were re-equipped with wartime Avengers which had been overhauled and updated. In 1955, a further eight Avengers entered Canadian service in the Airborne Early Warning role, carrying large and powerful equipment. New Zealand acquired two squadrons of Grumman Avengers, which were used as

dive-bombers by Nos.30 and 31 Squadrons. Secondary roles undertaken by the Kiwi Avengers included the spraying of Japanese gardens with diesel oil and target drogue towing.

Post-war, the type was also adapted to a wide variety of civilian uses, including crop-spraying and water-bombing. During 1947 an Avenger was used for trials of aerial seed-sowing and fertilizing in New Zealand. With an additional auxiliary fuel tank converted into a hopper installed in the bomb bay, it could carry 1017kg/2240lb of fertilizer.

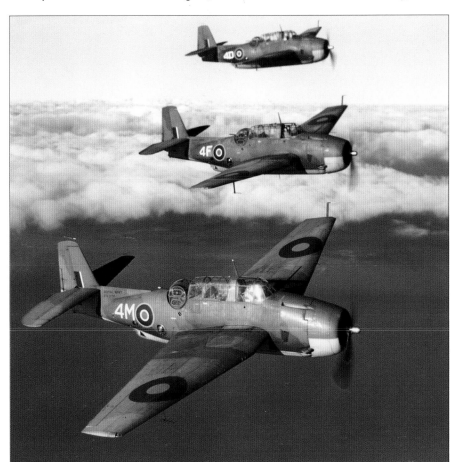

Grumman TBM-3 Avenger 🇺🇸

First flight: August 1, 1941

Power: One Wright 1900hp R-2600-20 radial engine

Armament: Two 12.7mm/0.5in fixed forward-firing machine-guns in the upper part of the forward fuselage, two trainable 7.62mm/0.3in machine-guns in rear cockpit; external bomb or depth charge load of 1021kg/2250lb

Size: Wingspan – 16.51m/54ft 2in
Length – 12.48m/40ft 11in
Height – 5m/16ft 5in
Wing area – 45.52m²/490sq ft
Weights: Empty – 4787kg/10,545lb
Maximum take-off – 8124kg/17,895lb

Performance: Maximum speed – 444kph/276 mph
Ceiling – 7625km/25,000ft
Range – 1609km/1000 miles
Climb – 328m/1075ft per minute

LEFT: **Three Avengers of No.846 Squadron, Fleet Air Arm, pictured in December 1943. Torpedo-armed British Avengers served until 1947, but anti-submarine versions flew on in Fleet Air Arm service until 1962.**

Handley Page Halifax

RAF Fighter Command's Hurricane was always overshadowed by the Spitfire, and in Bomber Command the Halifax was regularly eclipsed by the Lancaster, despite the Handley Page bomber's significant contribution to the Allied victory in World War II. The Halifax preceded the Lancaster into Bomber Command service and was the first four-engine RAF "heavy" to drop bombs on Germany in World War II.

TOP: **A Halifax II of No.35 Squadron (note the TL code on the aircraft), a unit of the Bomber Command Pathfinder Force (PFF). This aircraft, W7676, was lost on a raid on Nuremberg on the night of August 28–9, 1942.** ABOVE: **A clear illustration of the destruction caused by large, heavy bomber raids.**

Originally designed as a twin-engine monoplane to Specification P.13/36 using the ill-fated Rolls Royce Vulture engine, the Halifax underwent a radical redesign in 1937. The aircraft was uprated with four 1280hp Merlin X engines and defensive armament for the seven-man crew, which was comprised of two 7.7mm/0.303in Browning machine-guns in the nose turret, two in beam positions and four in the rear turret. The prototype first flew in October 1939, the first production aircraft entering service with RAF Bomber Command a year later with No.35 Squadron of No.4 Group. The Halifax's first bombing operation saw six aircraft of No.35 attack enemy targets in Le Havre, France, on the night of March 11–12, 1941.

The Halifax Mk I was built in three groups, Series I, II and III, the difference being the permitted take-off weight of each. The Series III also had an increased fuel capacity. The Mk II was again made in three series. The Series I was powered by four 1390hp Merlin XX engines and had increased fuel capacity. The two hand-held machine-guns in the aircraft's waist positions were deleted and replaced by a Boulton Paul twin-gun turret in the dorsal position. Flame-damping exhaust muffs were removed to improve performance, and the little-used nose turret was also eliminated. The Halifax II Series IA was powered by 1460hp Merlin 22 engines housed in low-drag cowlings. For forward defence, a single machine-gun was mounted through a redesigned Perspex nose cone and a four-gun low-drag dorsal turret was also fitted. Later production Series IA aircraft also introduced the rectangular vertical tail

RIGHT: **Life went on as normally as possible around RAF bomber bases. Here, a serviceman lends a hand with a pitchfork. In the background is DT807, a Halifax II built by the English Electric Company.**

surfaces that became synonymous with the Halifax. These modifications raised the aircraft's speed by 32kph/20mph compared with the Mk I.

The next major development was the Mk III model, which was powered by four 1615hp Bristol Hercules XVI radial engines. The first example flew in July 1943. Other modifications included a retractable tail wheel and an H2S radar scanner in a blister beneath the lower rear fuselage or a ventral gun as standard. On later production examples, extended wingtips were introduced, thereby raising the span to 31.76m/104ft 2in. This new wing was used on all subsequent Halifax variants. The Halifax Mk IV was a project only and by the time the ultimate Mk VI and VII bomber versions were produced in 1944, the Halifax was showing its age and very few were produced. In 1944 some Mk IIIs, Vs and VIIs were converted for paratroop-dropping and glider-towing in preparation for the D-Day offensive.

A total of 6176 aircraft were built and, although overshadowed by the Avro Lancaster, the Handley Page Halifax proved to be a far more versatile aircraft in that it could be adapted to many different roles. The Halifax squadrons of the RAF flew 82,773 operational sorties for the loss of 1884 aircraft (2.2 per cent) during World War II. The last Halifaxes were phased out of Royal Air Force and French Armée de l'Air service in 1952.

RIGHT: **A Halifax Mk I of No.76 Squadron.** BELOW: **An aircraft of No.10 Squadron. Although in the shadow of the "Lanc", the Halifax was produced in great numbers and played a key role in the ultimate Allied victory.**

Handley Page Halifax Mk III

First flight: October 25, 1939
Power: Four Bristol 1615hp Hercules VI or XVI 14-cylinder two-row radial engines
Armament: One 7.7mm/0.303in machine-gun in nose position, four 7.7mm/0.303in machine-guns each in dorsal and tail turrets; internal bomb load of 6,583kg/14,500lb
Size: Wingspan – 31.75m/104ft 2in
  Length – 21.82m/71ft 7in
  Height – 6.32m/20ft 9in
  Wing area – 118.45m²/1275sq ft
Weights: Empty – 17,706kg/39,000lb
  Maximum take-off – 30,872kg/68,000lb
Performance: Maximum speed – 454kph/282mph
  Ceiling – 7320m/24,000ft
  Range – 3194km/1985 miles
  Climb – 229m/750ft per minute

LEFT: **The squadron code "KM" identifies these Hampden Mk Is as aircraft of No.44 Squadron.**
BELOW: **Men of a No.83 Squadron Hampden leaving their aircraft after a flight early in World War II.**

Handley Page Hampden

The Handley Page Hampden prototype H.P.52 first flew in June 1936, and after Royal Air Force trials and various modifications, the type entered service with No.5 Group, RAF, during the summer of 1938. This five-seat medium bomber was so fast and manoeuvrable that Handley Page initially presented it to the RAF as a fighter-bomber. The pilot had a fixed forward-firing gun in addition to the aircraft's three manually operated Lewis guns for all-round defence. This defensive system gave the Hampden the edge over its British rivals because it didn't suffer from the drag and weight penalties of heavy gun turrets. In fact, the Hampden bomb load was almost equal to that carried by the bigger Whitley and Wellington, and it was almost as fast as the Blenheim medium bomber.

By the start of World War II, eight RAF squadrons were fully operational and took part in the early raids against German naval shore installations and shipping in the North Sea. However, daylight raid formations over enemy territory soon encountered opposition from fast German single-engine fighters, and the Hampden squadrons suffered heavy losses. In fact, casualties were so high that the Hampdens were taken off operations until they could be equipped with much better armament and armour. By then the decision had been taken that RAF Bomber Command would become mainly a night-raiding force, which no doubt saved many Hampden crews' lives.

Nicknamed the "Flying Suitcase" because of the cramped crew positions in a very narrow fuselage, the Hampden

had a successful career with No.5 Group during the summer of 1940, bombing Germany itself, mine-laying and bombing invasion barges in continental ports along the English Channel. It had a separate and successful career as a long-range torpedo bomber with RAF Coastal Command until late 1943.

A total of 1430 Hampden medium bombers were built before the type was replaced in RAF squadron service by the Avro Manchester from 1941.

Handley Page Hampden Mk II

First flight: June 21, 1936
Power: Two Bristol 1000hp Pegasus XVIII 9-cylinder radial engines
Armament: One 7.7mm/0.303in machine-gun in port side of forward fuselage, one in nose position, two in dorsal and two in ventral positions; bomb load of 1816kg/4000lb
Size: Wingspan – 21.08m/69ft 2in
Length – 16.33m/53ft 7in
Height – 4.55m/14ft 11in
Wing area – 62.06m²/668sq ft
Weights: Empty – 5348kg/11,780lb
Maximum take-off – 8515kg/18,756lb
Performance: Maximum speed – 409kph/254mph
Ceiling – 5795m/19,000ft
Range – 3034km/1885 miles
Climb – 300m/980ft per minute

LEFT: **Daylight raids early in the war showed that the Hampden had defensive deficiencies.**

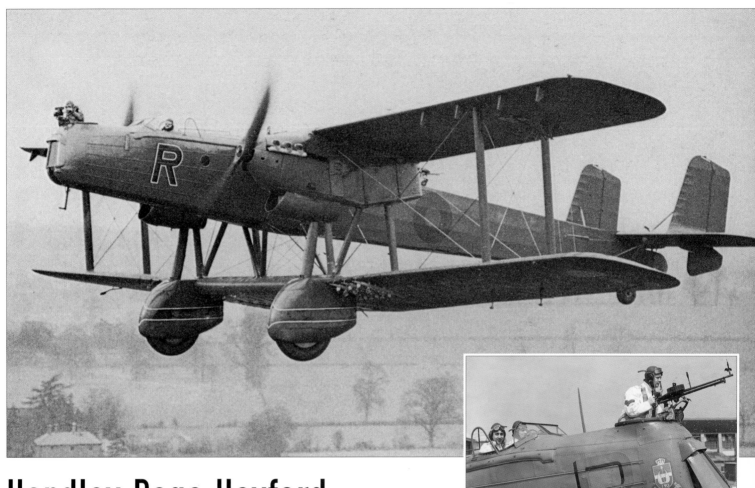

Handley Page Heyford

The Heyford was the last biplane bomber in RAF service and even looked dated when new, its fixed spatted landing gear doing nothing to improve its appearance. The Heyford's wings were of metal frame with fabric covering, while the fuselage was half metal (forward) and half fabric-covered. Despite this, the Heyford was the most important British bomber of the mid-1930s.

Three prototypes were ordered for evaluation in 1927, the first having its maiden flight in June 1930. Successful testing led to the type being ordered, and when production ended in July 1936, 15 Heyford Mk I, 21 Heyford Mk IA, 16 Heyford Mk II and 70 Heyford Mk III aircraft had been delivered. The marks differed little except in the type of engines installed, all Rolls-Royce Kestrels.

Perhaps the most striking visual feature of the bomber was that its fuselage was mounted on the upper wing. This gave the pilot and defensive gunners an excellent field of vision. To protect the aircraft's blind spot below and to the rear, a retractable ventral "dustbin" turret could be lowered from beneath the rear fuselage.

The centre section of the lower wing was thick enough to contain cells for the carriage of bombs. It is a matter of opinion if the proximity of the bomb cells to the ground made for speedy re-arming since armourers had to lie on the ground beneath the aircraft to secure the bombs in place.

The first unit to be equipped with the type in November 1933 was No.99 Squadron based at Upper Heyford. Nos.7, 9, 10, 38, 78, 97, 102, 148, 149 and 166 Squadrons followed.

As Whitleys and Wellesleys appeared from 1937, the Heyford was gradually phased out, the last being replaced by Wellingtons in 1939. The type continued to be used for training purposes until being finally retired in July 1941.

TOP: **K3500, Heyford I of 99 Squadron. The aircraft was lost after an engine failure at night in May 1937. Note the bomb shackles under the wing.**
ABOVE: **A Heyford crew of No.10 Squadron poses for the camera. The gunner's exposed position cannot have been a popular one.**

Handley Page Heyford Mk IA

First flight: June 1930 (prototype)
Power: Two Rolls-Royce 575hp Kestrel IIIS 12-cylinder piston engines
Armament: Three 7.7mm/0.303in machine-guns in nose, dorsal and ventral "dustbin" positions; up to 1589kg/3500lb bomb load
Size: Wingspan – 22.86m/75ft
  Length – 17.68m/58ft
  Height – 5.33m/17ft 6in
  Wing area – 136.56m²/1470sq ft
Weights: Empty – 4177kg/9200lb
  Maximum take-off – 7672kg/16,900lb
Performance: Maximum speed – 229kmh/142mph
  Ceiling – 6405m/21,000ft
  Range – 1481km/920 miles with reduced bomb load
  Climb – 213m/700ft per minute

Handley Page 0/400

Given that powered flight was so new, Handley Page's World War I series of large night-bombers was a remarkable achievement. The Handley Page 0/400 was a refinement of the earlier 0/100, which was designed to an Admiralty specification for a dedicated bomber aircraft – at the time (1914) this was a revolutionary idea. 0/100s were operational in France in 1916, and revision of the design (increased fuel capacity and better engines) led to the hugely successful 0/400 bomber. Five hundred and fifty were built in Britain and a further 100 were produced in the USA. The 0/400 was a very large aircraft, and in daylight would have been easy prey for capable German fighters. It was therefore used as a night-bomber and could carry ordnance up to the size of the 749kg/1650lb bomb, the heaviest used by the British during World War I.

Charged with attacking enemy industrial targets, the 0/400s would fly in fleets of up to 40 a night. These raids were the first true strategic bombing raids in history, and the large Handley Page bombers were seen by some military leaders as the future of waging war. More than 400 0/400s operated with the Royal Air Force before the Armistice of November 1918, equipping Nos. 58, 97, 115, 207, 214, 215 and 216 Squadrons of the RAF. In August 1918 an 0/400 was attached to No.1 Squadron of the Australian Flying Corps serving in the Middle East. No.1 worked with T.E. Lawrence, whose Arab associates, impressed by the sheer size of the aircraft, reportedly called it "The Father of all aeroplanes".

The type served in the RAF until late 1919, when it was replaced by the Vickers Vimy. Post-war, ten 0/400s were converted from military to civil configuration and used in the UK by Handley Page Transport Ltd.

ABOVE AND BELOW: **The 0/400 was a large aircraft, and the ability to fold back the wings on the ground made for easier stowage. The lone proud airman (below) gives a good idea of the aircraft's sheer size.**

Handley Page 0/400

First flight: December 17, 1915

Power: Two Rolls-Royce 360hp Eagle VIII Jupiter VIII piston engines

Armament: Various bomb loads, sixteen 50.8kg/112lb bombs or one 749kg/1650lb bomb, two 7.7mm/0.303 Lewis Guns in nose, two Lewis guns in mid-upper position, and single Lewis firing through lower rear trapdoor

Size: Wingspan – 30.48m/100ft
Length – 19.17m/62ft 10.75in
Height – 6.72m/22ft 0.75in
Wing area – 153.1m²/1648sq ft

Weights: Empty – 3859kg/8502lb
Maximum take-off – 6065kg/13,360lb

Performance: Maximum speed – 157kph/98mph
Service ceiling – 2590m/8500ft
Range – 1046km/650 miles
Climb – 3048m/10,000ft in 40 minutes

Hawker Typhoon

The Typhoon was designed around the new Rolls-Royce and Napier 24-cylinder 2000hp engine then under development, and flew for the first time in February 1940. Development and production problems delayed the Typhoon's delivery to the RAF until August 1941, when it became the RAF's first 643kph/400mph fighter. However, the extent of engine and structural problems in its early days was such that the large Hawker fighter was almost withdrawn from service. Instead, the problems were resolved and a use was found for the Typhoon's high low-level speed. Luftwaffe Focke-Wulf 190s had been carrying out hit-and-run raids along Britain's south coast, and the Typhoon, with its top speed of 663kph/412mph, was the only British fighter that could catch them. Typhoons destroyed four raiders within days of being deployed.

Following the success of night raids over occupied France in November 1942, the fighter was employed increasingly for offensive duties, strafing enemy airfields, shipping, roads, railways and bridges. From 1943, "Tiffies" went on the offensive, attacking targets in

France and the Low Countries, and when carrying rocket projectiles, they proved to be truly devastating aircraft.

Just prior to D-Day (June 6, 1944), Typhoons attacked German radar installations. These high-risk daylight attacks against heavily defended targets robbed the enemy of their radar "eyes" when they needed them most.

Relentless day and night attacks by RAF Typhoons on German communications targets greatly aided the D-Day operations. The aircraft that was once almost scrapped from RAF service eventually equipped no fewer than 26 squadrons of the 2nd Tactical Air Force. The Typhoon's original bomb load of 227kg/500lb gradually increased to 908kg/2000lb, the heaviest payload of any fighter-bomber. With eight 27.2kg/60lb rocket projectiles beneath the wing in which were buried four 20mm/0.78in cannon each firing 600 rounds per minute, at low level the "Tiffie" was a monster that harried German ground forces throughout Normandy. Later Typhoons had the bubble cockpit canopy in place of the earlier "glasshouse" framed cockpit, which improved visibility.

TOP AND ABOVE: **Although designed as a pure fighter, it will be as a ground-attack type that the Typhoon will perhaps be best remembered. The "Tiffie" inflicted massive damage on German forces before, during and after the D-Day landings. Note the rockets beneath the wing of the aircraft pictured immediately above.**

Hawker Typhoon IB

First flight: May 27, 1941 (Production IA)

Power: Napier 2180hp Sabre IIA 24-cylinder sleeve-valve liquid cooled piston engine

Armament: Four 20mm/0.78in cannon in outer wings and racks for eight rockets or two 227kg/500lb bombs

Size: Wingspan – 12.67m/41ft 7in
  Length – 9.73m/31ft 11in
  Height – 4.67m/15ft 4in
  Wing area – 25.92m²/279sq ft

Weights: Empty – 3995kg/8800lb
  Maximum take-off – 6015kg/13,250lb

Performance: Maximum speed – 663kph/412mph
  Ceiling – 10,736m/35,200ft
  Range – 821km/510 miles (with bombs)
  Climb – 914m/3000ft per minute

Heinkel He111

The prototype of the Heinkel He111 first flew in February 1935 and owed many of its design features to the earlier single-engine He70 which set eight world speed records in 1933. Designed in 1934 as a twin-engine high-speed transport and revealed to the world as a civil airliner in 1935, the He111 was in fact secretly developed as the world's most advanced medium bomber. Six He111 C-series airliners went into service with Lufthansa in 1936 but even the airliner versions served a military purpose, as two He111s in Lufthansa markings flew secret photographic reconnaissance missions over the Soviet Union, France and Britain.

It took the installation of 1000hp Daimler-Benz DB 600A engines and the improved all-round performance they bestowed to make the He111 a viable military aircraft. The first mass-produced bomber versions, the He111 E and He111 F, were desperately effective in the testing-ground that was the Spanish Civil War, where, as part of the Condor Legion, they flew in support of the Fascists. The effectiveness of Blitzkrieg tactics was due in no small part to the Heinkel bomber – the bombing of Guernica sent a clear message around the world about the military might of the Luftwaffe. The speed of the He111 enabled it to outpace many of the fighter aircraft pitted against it in Spain, but this led the Germans to assume incorrectly that their bombers would reign supreme in the European war that was to come.

ABOVE AND BELOW: **A German bomber, built in Spain post-war, powered by British engines. These aircraft were Spanish licence-built CASA 2.111s, and served the Spanish Air Force into the 1960s. These were the "Heinkels" that appeared in the film "Battle of Britain".**

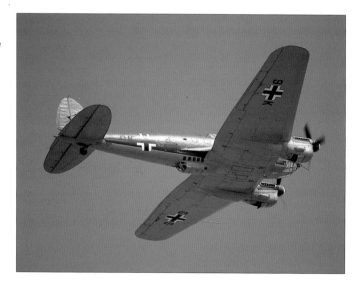

However, the Heinkel's shortcomings were exposed when it came up against the more modern fighters of the Royal Air Force – the Spitfire and the Hurricane. Although by sheer weight of numbers, the He111s did inflict much destruction on Britain during the early stages of World War II, losses mounted and the Heinkel was soon restricted to night operations and other specialized missions.

Under cover of darkness during the Blitz of 1940–1, the He111 continued to perform as an effective bomber, inflicting serious blows against its British enemies, including the devastating raids on Coventry.

Due to a German decision to focus on mass production of existing weapons rather than invest in development of newer ones, the He111 laboured on long after it should have been retired. He111s were developed for use as torpedo bombers, glider tugs and troop transports, and in the last year of the war they served as air launch platforms for V1 flying bombs targeted against British cities. Perhaps the strangest development of the He111 was the joining of two aircraft at the wing, with an additional section of wing containing a fifth engine. Twelve examples of this truly strange-looking aircraft were produced as tow aircraft for the large Messerschmitt Me321 transport gliders. By the end of World War II, however, the He111 was used mainly as a transport aircraft.

By the end of 1944, over 7300 He111s had been built for the Luftwaffe, while a further 236 were licence-built by the Spanish manufacturer CASA. The Spanish machines (designated CASA 2.111) were identical to the He111 H-6 produced in Germany and half were powered by Junkers engines supplied from Germany. The rest of the Spanish aircraft, built post-war, had Rolls-Royce Merlin engines. Spain continued to operate the Heinkel bombers until 1965.

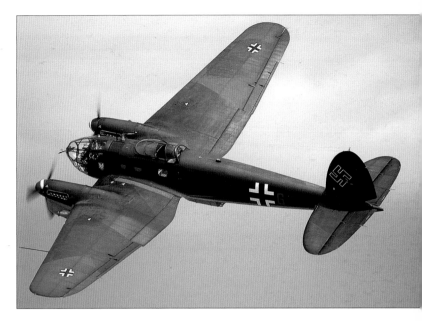

ABOVE RIGHT: **The Spanish machines were the same as the He111 H-6.** RIGHT: **The real thing – a formation of Luftwaffe He111s.** BELOW: **Groundcrew attending to a Luftwaffe He111 early in World War II.**

Heinkel He111 H-16

First flight: February 24, 1935 (prototype)

Power: Two Junkers 1350hp Jumo 211F piston engines

Armament: One 20mm/0.78in MG FF cannon in nose, one 13mm/0.51in MG131 gun in dorsal position, two 7.92mm/0.31in MG15 guns in rear of ventral gondola and two 7.92mm/0.31in MG81 guns in each of two beam positions; up to 2500kg/5503lb of bombs carried internally and externally

Size: Wingspan – 22.60m/74ft 1in
Length – 16.40m/53ft 9in
Height – 4m/13ft1in
Wing area – 86.50m²/931.07sq ft

Weights: Empty – 8680kg/19,105lb
Maximum take-off – 14,000kg/30,814lb

Performance: Maximum speed – 436kph/271mph
Service ceiling – 8390m/27,500ft
Range – 1950km/1212 miles
Climb – 4500m/14,765ft in 30 minutes

Heinkel He177

Had the Nazis produced an atomic bomb, as the Luftwaffe's only heavy bomber it was the He177 Greif (griffon) that would have carried it. At the end of World War II a sole aircraft undergoing modification for the role was discovered in Czechoslovakia. Given the number of these aircraft that had to turn back from missions due to engine problems, the bomb might have posed more of a threat to Germany than anywhere else. Of all the aircraft in the Luftwaffe's World War II inventory, the He177 had the greatest military potential and caused the greatest amount of trouble to its air and ground crews.

In many ways, it is surprising that the aircraft made it to production at all because it was proposed to meet a baffling 1938 requirement for a large, long-range heavy bomber and anti-shipping aircraft that could deliver a sizeable 2000kg/ 4402lb bomb load in medium-angle dive-bombing attacks. It has to be borne in mind that while the Allies embraced the concept of strategic air power as a means of waging war, the Luftwaffe was always a tactical air power adjunct to German land forces. That different philosophy explained the lack of large, heavy bombers in the wartime Luftwaffe.

RIGHT AND BELOW: **Having emerged from an ill-considered specification, the He177 proved to be the only German four-engined "heavy" of World War II. In mid-1944, there were raids on the Eastern Front of up to 90 of these troublesome aircraft.**

At a glance, the six-seat He177 has two engines, but on closer inspection each Daimler-Benz DB-610 engine is in fact a pair of coupled DB605 engines driving a single propeller shaft. The designers decided that was a good way to reduce drag, but any benefits were far outweighed by the innumerable problems caused by these troublesome engines which regularly caught fire in the air, even at cruising speeds. Six out of the eight prototypes crashed and out of the first 35 pre-production A-0 models, built mainly by Arado, many were written off through take-off accidents or fires in flight. A further 130 A-1 versions were built by Arado, while Heinkel were responsible for the production of the A-3 and A-5 versions, of which 170 and 826 respectively were constructed.

The aircraft itself was essentially a good design, and the slim tubular fuselage and long wings gave a range of 5500km/3417 miles – far beyond anything else in the Luftwaffe inventory. The engine was the design's Achilles

heel, and plagued its service record. The type in A-1 form was first used in action by KG (*Kampfgeschwader*) 40 for maritime strike and reconnaissance missions from bases in France. The aircraft could carry an impressive range of anti-shipping ordnance, including the Henschel Hs 293 missile, which was guided after launch to its target by the bombardier's joystick in the gondola beneath the nose. The missile "pilot" followed the missile's course thanks to flares at the rear of the missile. Torpedoes and sea mines could also be deployed.

During January to March 1944 the Luftwaffe's KG40 and KG100 carried out what were known as the Steinbock raids. These revenge raids were in response to the Allies' escalating attacks against German cities and were aimed at London. The

planners knew the single most effective way that the aircraft could attack and hope to evade interception by the Royal Air Force's increasingly efficient nightfighter force. The aircraft climbed to around 9000m/29,527ft over the coast of Europe and then, at full power, began a shallow dive towards Britain. By the time the aircraft were over England they were at speeds of around 700kph/435mph, which made the aircraft hard to catch but did little for bombing accuracy. The raids were ineffective and although of the 35 aircraft that took part in the numerous raids only four were destroyed by British defences, many had to turn back repeatedly with engine fires and other malfunctions.

Following the D-Day landings, He177 anti-shipping missions from France ceased, but the type was still in use as a missile launch platform against the Allies in early 1945.

On the Eastern Front, KG4 and KG50 were first to use the He117 in the pure bomber role, and some aircraft were also fitted with huge 50mm/2in or even 75mm/2.93in anti-tank guns.

ABOVE: **An He117 A-5/R2 carrying a Henschel Hs 293A anti-shipping missile. The weapon could be carried on a special pylon fitted beneath the forward bomb bay or beneath the wing.** RIGHT AND BELOW: **The RAF evaluated certain captured enemy aircraft. Note that in both these photographs the Luftwaffe markings have been overpainted with RAF roundels, and broad D-Day invasion-type stripes have been applied to the wings and rear fuselage to deter friendly would-be attackers. The aircraft pictured on the right has had "Prise de Guerre" painted on its side.**

Heinkel He177 A-5

First flight: November 19, 1939
Power: Two Daimler-Benz 2950hp DB 610A piston engines
Armament: Three 7.92mm/0.31in machine-guns, three 13mm/0.51in machine-guns and two 20mm/0.78in cannon in nose, tail, dorsal and ventral gondola positions; up to 1000kg/2201lb of bombs and two anti-shipping missiles
Size: Wingspan – 31.44m/103ft 1.75in
Length – 20.4m/66ft 11.25in
Height – 6.39m/20ft 11.75in
Wing area – 102m²/1097.95sq ft
Weights: Empty – 16,800kg/36,976lb
Maximum take-off – 31,000kg/68,231lb
Performance: Maximum speed – 490kph/304mph
Ceiling – 8000m/26,245ft
Range – 5500km/3417 miles
Climb – 260m/853ft per minute

Ilyushin Il-2 Shturmovik

During the 1930s, the Soviet government was very interested in developing a dedicated purpose-designed anti-tank aircraft. Various projects came to nothing, then in 1938, as war seemed inevitable, a team under Sergei V. Ilyushin at the Soviet Central Design Bureau (TsKB) produced a new design, a two-seat aircraft designated the TsKB-55 which first flew in December 1939. The Ilyushin design was then redesignated BSh-2, for Bronirovanni Shturmovik or Armoured Assault Aircraft. Although some of the aircraft, now designated Il-2, did reach front-line units by the time of the June 1941 German invasion, the new and unfamiliar aircraft had little impact. By now the Soviets were concerned that many of

ABOVE AND BELOW LEFT: **More Il-2s were built than any other aircraft in history. When told of production problems with the type, Stalin said the tough, hard-hitting aircraft were "needed by the Red Army like it needs air or bread". The large hollow above the engine directed air to the engine's radiator intake.**

their aircraft factories might be overrun by the Germans, so development and production of the Il-2 ceased while the factories were relocated beyond the Urals. This was a massive undertaking, and all the more remarkable because Il-2s were coming off the new refined production lines only two months after the relocation of the production facilities.

This heavily-armoured ground-attack monoplane was the backbone of the Soviet ground-attack units during World War II and was one of the most formidable aircraft used in the conflict. Perhaps the key to the aircraft's success was its survivability due to the extraordinary amounts of protective armour which was not installed but was part of the aircraft's structure itself, guarding the pilot, engine, fuel tank, cooling system and bomb bays.

The aircraft first flew in single-seat form on October 12, 1940, and went on to be the most produced aircraft in history, with more than 36,000 built. The heavily armoured Il-2 reached front-line units in May 1941. Though devastating against ground targets, the aircraft was no match for modern fighter aircraft when Soviet fighter cover was not available, and it suffered heavy losses from the Luftwaffe. The solution was proposed in February 1942 – the two-seat II-2m3, which was in fact the original configuration proposed by Ilyushin. The second crewman manned a 12.7mm/0.5in machine-gun for rear protection but he was not as protected by armour as the pilot and was seven times more likely to be killed in action. The forward-firing armament of two 20mm/0.78in cannon was also replaced by two high-velocity 23mm/0.9in cannon.

On November 19, 1942, the Red Army launched a counterattack against the German offensive in Stalingrad, and their white Shturmoviks were the masters of the air. Over the following four days the II-2s carried out around 1000 sorties attacking German armour, artillery and troops. The Ilyushin aircraft was a key part of the Soviet counterattack which led to the German surrender at Stalingrad on February 2, 1943.

The II-2m3 had four small bomb bays that could carry up to 192 2.5kg/5.5lb PTAB anti-tank bomblets which the aircraft would scatter over enemy columns. It was also equipped with the DAG-10 grenade launcher which would eject small aerial mines on parachutes in the path of pursuing aircraft.

By mid-1943, Shturmovik pilots had perfected their tactics. Flying in groups of eight to twelve aircraft in open country, they would attack soft targets such as personnel or soft-skinned vehicles by simply skimming in as low as 5m/16ft. Against armoured columns, they would attack straight down the column or weave across it repeatedly, scattering the PTAB anti-tank bombs from as low as 100m/320ft. Bunkers or emplacements were attacked using dive-bombing techniques. To tackle armour formations on a battlefield, the II-2s would form their "circle of death" above and around the enemy below. Aircraft would peel off it, turn and attack the tanks below almost at their leisure, knowing that a large part of the sky above was protected by the encircling II-2s. Ground fire less than 20mm/0.78in calibre held no fear for the well-armoured Shturmoviks. The attacks would continue until the aircraft expended fuel and ammunition.

The II-2's contribution to the pivotal Soviet victory at Kursk was considerable. The aircraft destroyed 70 tanks of the 9th Panzer Division in just 20 minutes, killed 2000 men and destroyed 270 tanks of the 3rd Panzer Division in just two hours, and virtually wiped out the 17th Panzer Division.

TOP AND ABOVE: **The rear gunner of II-2m3 frequently had the aft cockpit canopy removed to improve his or her field of fire. The aircraft in the foreground immediately above bears the legend "Avenger".** BELOW LEFT: **The II-10 replaced the II-2 in production in 1944. With fighter-like handling, the II-10 was a major redevelopment of the II-2, which remained in service in the Eastern Bloc into the late 1950s.**

Ilyushin II-2m3 Shturmovik

First flight: March 1941 (production II-2)

Power: One Mikulin 1720hp Am-38F piston engine

Armament: Two 23mm/0.9in wing-mounted machine-guns and one 12.7mm/0.5in machine-gun for gunner; up to six 100kg/220lb bombs or two 250kg/551lb bombs plus eight rocket projectiles under outer wing

Size: Wingspan – 14.6m/47ft 10.75in
Length – 11.65m/38ft 2.5in
Height – 4.17m/13ft 8in
Wing area – 38.5m²/414.42sq ft

Weights: Empty – 4525kg/9959lb
Maximum take-off – 6360kg/13,998lb

Performance: Maximum speed – 410kph/255mph
Service ceiling – 6000m/19,690ft
Range – 765km/475 miles
Climb – 5000m/16,405ft in 12 minutes

Ilyushin Il-4

Always overshadowed by its Western counterparts, the Il-4 was produced in great quantities, and was one of the best bomber aircraft of World War II. It was derived from the Ilyushin DB-3, a record-breaking long-range bomber that first flew in prototype form in 1935. The second prototype, the TsKB-30, amazed the world when it flew from Moscow to Canada, a distance of 8000km/4971 miles. The DB-3 served in great numbers with the Long Range Aviation and Naval Aviation elements of the Soviet Air Force, and carried out early bombing raids on Germany in World War II. The 7.62mm/0.3in rifle-calibre armament of the DB-3 proved inadequate against Finnish fighters in the 1939–40 Winter War, but was never significantly improved.

An improved version, the DB-3F, was developed in 1938, one of the requirements being that assembly was to be very straightforward for mass production. The new version bore little resemblance to its predecessor, having a streamlined and extensively glazed nose. It was also more heavily armoured than its predecessor, more so when it saw action because the gunners proved to be a popular target for enemy fighter pilots.

Test-flights were concluded by June 1939 and the type, redesignated Il-4 in 1940, was ordered into production. After the German invasion, production had been disrupted by moving the lines to the safety of Siberia. During the production run in 1942, wood was introduced in place of some metal components made of scarce light alloys. Metal was reintroduced as soon as it became available. Manufacture of the Il-4 continued until 1944, by which time 5256 had been built.

TOP AND ABOVE: **The Ilyushin DB-3 bomber was a record-breaker, and its defensive armament (7.62mm/0.3in) was one of the aircraft's few shortcomings.**

A fourth crew member, the "hatch" gunner, was added to improve defence, and two external fuel tanks were also added, which resulted in an 18 per cent increase in the fuel and an additional 600km/373 mile range. The outer wing was redesigned with leading-edge sweepback, thus improving stability and control. New, more efficient propellers and bigger split-flaps were installed to improve short-field operations.

The Il-4 was used for long-range bombing missions, but was equally efficient hauling its maximum bomb load of 2500kg/5502lb over short distances to attack tactical targets. The first Soviet bombing raid on Berlin was carried out by naval Il-4s on the night of August 8–9, 1941.

LEFT: **The upper gun turret of the DB-3F was fitted with a 12.7mm/0.5in machine-gun.** BELOW: **These aircraft were the backbone of Soviet long-range bomber capability.**

ABOVE: **The Il-4 proved itself to be among the best bomber aircraft produced by the Soviet Union in World War II. Note the very thick flying suits worn by the crew in this photograph, and also the machine-gun in the centre of the aircraft's nose.**

Il-4 crewman Lieutenant I.M. Chisov was thrown clear of his exploding aircraft following a German fighter attack in January 1942. Without a parachute, he fell 6710m/22,000ft into a snow-filled ravine and, though badly injured, lived to tell the tale.

The Il-4 was also developed as a mining and torpedo bomber equipped with a 940kg/2069lb torpedo for attacks against German shipping in the Baltic. Some pilots were happy to carry two of these heavy weapons at the same time. These naval Il-4s were also equipped with six RS-82 rocket projectiles beneath the wing for suppression of flak ships and other defences.

The type remained in Soviet military use after the end of World War II into the 1950s, and was given the NATO codename "Bob". An improved version, the Il-6, was designed for high-altitude operations powered by two 1500hp diesel engines, but was never flown.

Ilyushin Il-4

First flight: 1939
Power: Two 1100hp M-88B radial piston engines
Armament: One 12.7mm/0.5in and two 7.62mm/
0.3in machine-guns on mounts in nose and
dorsal positions; up to 2500kg/5502lb bomb
load
Size: Wingspan – 21.44m/70ft 4.25in
Length – 14.8m/48ft 6.75in
Height – 4.1m/13ft 5.5in
Wing area – 66.7m²/717.98sq ft
Weights: Empty – 5800kg/12,766lb
Maximum take-off – 11,300kg/24,871lb
Performance: Maximum speed – 430kph/267mph
Ceiling – 9700m/31825ft
Range – 3800km/2361 miles
Climb – 270m/886ft per minute

Junkers Ju 52/3m

The Junkers Ju 52/3m is one of the greatest aircraft ever built. Though simple and unwieldy by modern standards, with a fixed undercarriage and corrugated construction, the robust Junkers was built in great numbers and served in a variety of roles from bomber to ski-equipped airliner. It equipped no fewer than 30 airlines pre-war and remained in service with a Swiss airline half a century after the type first flew.

The 3m (for three engines or *Motoren*) was developed from a single-engine version of the same aircraft, the Ju 52. The 3m version first flew in April 1932 and quickly became the standard aircraft of Lufthansa, accounting for three-quarters of its fleet. The military applications of this rugged and capable aircraft were clear to the German militarists, who encouraged the development of a military bomber-transport version. The Ju 52/3mg3e, powered by three BMW 525hp 132A-3 engines, could carry six 100kg/220lb bombs. It had a faired gun position on top of the fuselage rear of the wing and a primitive "dustbin" turret, each mounting a 7.92mm/0.31in machine-gun. As a transport, it could carry 18 troops or 12 stretchers.

This version became the first type to equip the first bomber group of the fledgling and secretly developing Luftwaffe, and it debuted as a bomber in 1936 during the Spanish Civil War with Germany's Condor Legion. Initially the Junkers ferried more than 10,000 Moroccan troops to Spain in support of the

TOP: **The "Tante Ju" (Auntie) Junkers, developed throughout its service, was the aerial workhorse of Nazi Germany.** ABOVE: **The Ju 52/3m was the standard airliner of Lufthansa, making up most of its fleet in the mid-1930s. The aircraft pictured here is still operated by the German airline and appears at air shows around Europe.**

Fascists, but then began bombing Republican targets and supporting ground troops battling for control of Madrid.

In March 1937 the Ju 52s, which were then considered to be slow, were tasked with night-time bombing of Republican-held territory. For the rest of the war the Ju 52 was used for moving large numbers of troops and supplies. That said, by the end of the war the Junkers bombers had dropped 6096 tonnes/6000 tons of bombs – the Ju 52 had played an important part in Franco's victory.

By the outbreak of World War II, the Ju 52 was obsolete as a bomber but was used on a vast scale as a transport aircraft. Over 1000 Ju 52s were in service with the Luftwaffe

LEFT: **The Ju 52 had a fixed undercarriage – one of its recognition features, together with the type's corrugated metal skin.**

ABOVE LEFT: **Each aircraft in this formation of Ju 52s has its ventral "dustbin" gun turret deployed – another unpopular gunner position.** ABOVE: **The type was improved constantly (the aircraft shown here has streamlined housings over the wheels), and appeared in a multitude of versions.**

at the start of World War II, but at peak, around 5000 examples of the rugged workhorse were used by the Third Reich. Hitler himself used a Ju 52 as his private transport for a time. Ju 52s transported the attacking army and their supplies during the German invasions of Norway, Denmark, France and the Low Countries in 1940.

In May 1941, around 500 Ju 52s took part in the huge airborne assault by the Germans on the island of Crete. Numerous versions appeared during the war with improved radio equipment, auto pilot and different self-defence armament. Minesweeper and glider tug versions also saw service. The Ju 52 was used on all fronts on which the Third Reich fought, and was a vital part of the Nazi war machine.

However, production of the aircraft was not limited to Germany. In post-war France, 400 examples of a version designated the AAC 1 Toucan were built, a number of them serving in the French Air Force and Navy. These French machines saw active service in the Algerian and Indo-China conflicts. Meanwhile in Spain CASA, who also produced a version of the Heinkel He111, built 170 aircraft designated C-352-L. An often forgotten Ju 52 fact is that ten reconditioned examples captured from the Luftwaffe flew with British European Airways in the immediate post-war years.

Junkers Ju 52/3mg3e

First flight: October 13, 1930 (Ju 52 single-engine version)

Power: Three BMW 725hp 132A-3 radial piston engines

Armament: One 7.92mm/0.31in machine-gun each in dorsal position and retractable ventral "dustbin" turret; 500kg/1100lb bomb load

Size: Wingspan – 29.24m/95ft 11.5in
Length – 18.9m/62ft
Height – 5.55m/18ft 2.5in
Wing area – 110.5m²/1189sq ft

Weights: Empty – 5720kg/12,589lb
Maximum take-off – 10,500kg/23,110lb

Performance: Maximum speed – 265kph/165mph
Service ceiling – 5900m/19,360ft
Range – 1000km/620 miles
Climb – 3000m/9840ft in 17 minutes, 30 seconds

TOP: **Shortly before World War II began, the new Ju 87B had re-equipped all Luftwaffe Stukageschwaden.** ABOVE: **Evaluated under combat conditions in Spain, the Stuka became a key aircraft in the Blitz strategy.**

Junkers Ju 87 Stuka

The Stuka (short for *Sturzkampfflugzeug* or dive-bomber) is one of the best-known wartime Luftwaffe-combat types and certainly the easiest to recognize with its inverted gull wings and fixed undercarriage. Like many Luftwaffe aircraft, the Ju 87 was designed to provide tactical support to the army in land actions.

Although dive-bombing was used as an attack technique in World War I, no aircraft in that conflict was specifically designed for the role. Junkers developed the first dedicated dive-bomber, the K47, in the 1920s and test-flew the aircraft in 1928. Most of these aircraft were exported to China amidst great secrecy because Germany was still bound by the post-World War I agreement that it should not be producing weapons of war.

German strategists saw the potential of the dive-bomber as an effective weapon when used in close support of ground forces, reducing the enemy's resistance before ground forces advanced. Still amidst great secrecy, Germany decided to manufacture dedicated dive-bomber aircraft, and in 1933 Henschel developed the Hs123 while Junkers continued to work on their K47. The Henschel design was a biplane, but the Ju 87 (derived from the K47) was a single-engine monoplane which broke with the Junkers tradition of corrugated skin construction. The prototype was powered, ironically as later events proved, by a Rolls-Royce Kestrel engine, and had its

maiden flight in May 1935. The Luftwaffe were very impressed by the potent new dive-bomber and, with testing complete, the Stuka began to enter service in 1937. These early Stukas were sent to Spain and the Civil War for operational evaluation with the German Condor Legion.

In the first production version, the Ju 87A-1, a single fin replaced the two of the prototype, dive brakes were fitted to the outer wings, and the British engine was replaced by a Junkers Jumo 210Ca 640hp engine. The A-2 model can be identified by the larger undercarriage fairings and was powered by the supercharged 680hp Jumo 210Da.

By early 1939, all the A-series aircraft were relegated to training duties, and all dive-bomber units began equipping with the more powerful Ju 87B series, powered by the 1200hp

Jumo 211Da direct-injection engine. More streamlined spats over the landing gear appeared, and the latest Stukas were now equipped with an automatic dive control. The B-2 was improved further and could carry up to 1000kg/2200lb of bombs. The D-series fitted with the 1410hp Jumo 211J-1 engine introduced more armour to protect the crew. Various sub-types saw action, including night ground-attack versions armed with cannon. From 1942, the Ju 87G-1 dedicated anti-tank version was in action on the Eastern Front.

The Stuka's automatic dive control enabled the pilot to pre-set a pull-out height should he black out in the course of a steep dive-bombing attack. On commencing the dive attack, the pilot adjusted the dive angle manually by referring to red indicator lines painted on the canopy showing 60, 75 and 80 degrees from horizontal. The pilot would visually aim the aircraft at his target until a signal light on the altimeter illuminated, telling the pilot to press the bomb-release button on the top of the control column. The automatic pull-out would commence as the bombs left their cradles. The bombs would

follow the same course to the target as the aircraft had during its dive, while the pilot would experience around 6g as the aircraft automatically levelled out to begin its climb skywards.

The rear gunner operated a machine-gun which might keep defending fighters at a safe distance, but a Stuka was easy prey for fast modern fighters. With air superiority achieved and against obsolete fighters in Poland and the Low Countries the Stuka was able to hold its own, but when it came up against the Hurricanes and Spitfires of the RAF large numbers were destroyed on cross-Channel missions. The Ju 87 had a slow top speed and could not climb away quickly. Accordingly, it was withdrawn from operations against the UK, but the type continued to serve in Greece, Crete, North Africa, Malta and on the Eastern Front.

The Stuka was more than a dive-bomber – it was also a psychological weapon. The wheel covers were fitted with sirens that would wind up as the aircraft went into their dive – this created terror among the enemy below. Whistles were also known to be fitted on to the fins of the bombs to ensure a similar effect as the ordnance fell. The total number of Stukas produced was around 5700 aircraft.

ABOVE: **A D-series Stuka, complete with extra armour for crew protection.**

RIGHT: **A Ju 87B, the version which introduced automatic dive control.**

BELOW: **Unmistakable with its inverted gull wings – the Stuka.**

Junkers Ju 87D-1

First flight: 1940

Power: One Junkers 1410hp Jumo 12-cylinder piston engine

Armament: Two 7.92mm/0.3in machine-guns in wings and two in rear cockpit; up to 1800kg/3962lb bomb load

Size: Wingspan – 13.8m/45ft 3.5in
Length – 11.5mm/37ft 8.75in
Height – 3.9m/12ft 9.5in
Wing area – 31.9m²/343.38sq ft

Weights: Empty – 3900kg/8584lb
Maximum take-off – 6600kg/14,526lb

Performance: Maximum speed – 410kph/255mph
Ceiling – 7290m/23,915ft
Range – 1535km/954 miles
Climb – 5000m/16,405ft in 19 minutes, 48 seconds

Junkers Ju 88

Said by many to be the most important German bomber of World War II, the Ju 88 was in front-line service from the start to the end of the war. The Ju 88 is widely described as the "German Mosquito", because like the de Havilland aircraft, the Ju 88 was an extremely versatile design and was developed from a bomber for use in the dive-bomber, torpedo-bomber, close support, reconnaissance, heavy fighter and nightfighter roles.

In January 1936, the ReichsLuftMinisterium (RLM, the German Air Ministry) released specifications for a new fast bomber that could carry a bomb load of over 500kg/1100lb. The Junkers Flugzeug und Motorenwerke company responded with the Junkers Ju 88, designed largely by two American nationals employed for their expertise in stressed-skin construction. Construction of the prototype began in May 1936 with the first flight of the Ju 88-V1 taking place on December 21, 1936. A total of five prototypes were built, and one, the Ju 88-V5, made several record-breaking speed flights. In 1937, the specification was modified to include dive-bombing capabilities as well as an increased payload and range. The Ju 88-V6 was the first prototype built to meet the new specification, and it flew on June 18, 1938. In the autumn of 1938, the RLM chose the Ju 88 to become the latest bomber to join the Luftwaffe, and the Ju 88A production version began to reach front-line units in 1939. When war did eventually break out in September 1939, it was the Ju88A-1

TOP: **The Ju 88 was without doubt the most versatile aircraft operated by the Luftwaffe in World War II, and was in production throughout the conflict.**
ABOVE: **The fastest of the principal German bombers, the Ju 88 was found to have poor defensive armament.**

that entered service, although the first recorded mission was not flown until later in that month. The arrival of the Ju 88 was a significant boost to Germany's bomber forces, and although it was heavier than both the Dornier Do17 and the Heinkel He111, even when it carried a substantial bomb load, it was still the fastest of the three. Unlike other Luftwaffe bomber types such as the Heinkel He111, the Ju 88 was not battle-tested in the Spanish Civil War.

The strong and manoeuvrable Ju 88 was a key Luftwaffe aircraft in the 1940 Battle of Britain but in spite of its speed, it suffered at the guns of the faster British fighters. Although the Ju 88 had an extensive battery of machine-guns for defence, all forward machine-guns except that operated by the pilot had to be operated by the flight engineer who had to leap from one gun to another as British fighters assaulted the aircraft. As a result of combat experiences, the bomber was modified to carry extra defensive guns as well as more armour to protect the crew.

The A-series was the standard bomber version of the Ju 88. About 20 Ju 88As were sold to Finland in 1939, and mass production of the Ju 88 started in 1940 with the A4. Large numbers of the Ju 88A-4 were built with longer wings to carry heavier bomb loads of up to 2500 or 3000kg/5502 or 6603lb. Despite this, the 88 continued to operate successfully from rough fields. By the end of the war, 17 different subtypes of the Ju 88A had been designed. One of the most bizarre came from a 1944 RLM request to Junkers to develop a composite aircraft consisting of a fighter aircraft mounted on top of an unmanned heavy bomber aircraft. This Mistel combination aircraft was then flown to the target, where the fighter's pilot released the bomber, which was filled with explosives and plummeted to earth while the fighter returned to base. These Mistel weapons used old Ju 88s coupled to Messerschmitt Bf109s or Focke-Wulf Fw190s. About 85 Mistel combinations were built by the end of the war but only a few missions were flown.

ABOVE: **The aircraft pictured here is a Ju 88A-5. Bombing, dive-bombing, nightfighting and reconnaissance were all roles carried out by the great varieties of Ju 88s produced during the war.**

RIGHT: **A Ju 88A-4 pictured over the Eastern Front in 1943.**
BELOW: **The large "glasshouse" nose of the Ju 88 gave the crew excellent forward vision.**

Junkers Ju 88A-4

First flight: December 21, 1936 (Ju 88 prototype)

Power: Two Junkers Jumo 1340hp 211J-1 piston engines

Armament: One 7.9mm/0.308in machine-gun in front cockpit, one 13mm/0.51in or two 7.9mm/0.308in machine-guns in front nose, two rearward-firing 7.9mm/0.308in machine-guns in rear cockpit and one 13mm/0.51in or two 7.9mm/0.308in machine-guns at rear of gondola beneath nose; up to 3600kg/7923lb carried internally and externally

Size: Wingspan – 20m/65ft 7in
Length – 14.4m/47ft 2.6in
Height – 4.85m/15ft 11in
Wing area – 54.5m²/586.6sq ft

Weights: Empty – 9860kg/21,041lb
Maximum take-off – 14,000kg/30,814lb

Performance: Maximum speed – 433kph/269mph
Ceiling – 8200m/26,900ft
Range – 2730km/1696 miles
Climb – 400m/1312ft per minute

Kawanishi H8K

When Japan first went to war with the Allies, its standard maritime patrol flying boat was the Kawanishi H6K. The type performed well in the early stages of the war in the reconnaissance and bombing roles until it came up against Allied fighters, when it suffered severe maulings. It had entered service in 1938 and, thinking ahead, the Japanese Navy immediately issued a specification for a replacement with a 30 per cent higher speed and 50 per cent greater range.

The requirement called for a long-range aircraft with better performance than Britain's Short Sunderland or the American Sikorsky XPBS-1. The designers produced one of the finest military flying boats ever built, and certainly the best of World War II.

To give the aircraft the required range, it carried eight small unprotected fuel tanks in the wings and a further six large tanks in the fuselage or, more correctly, hull. The hull tanks were partially self-sealing and also boasted a carbon dioxide fire extinguisher system. Ingeniously, the tanks were placed so that if any leaked, the fuel would collect in a fuel

TOP: **The H8K entered Imperial Japanese Navy service in late 1941 and first flew into action in March the following year.** ABOVE: **Fitted with beaching gear, this H8K, codenamed "Emily" by the Allies, is undergoing engine runs.**

"bilge" and then be pumped to an undamaged tank. The aircraft was a flying fuel tank, with 15,816 litres/3479 gallons being a typical fuel load and accounting for some 29 per cent of the take-off weight. The aircraft positively bristled with defensive armament – 20mm/0.78in cannons were carried in powered nose, dorsal and tail turrets, with two more in opposite beam blisters. A further three 7.7mm/0.303in machine-guns were in port and starboard beam hatches and in the ventral position. The crew positions were well armoured.

ABOVE: **The H8K was the fastest flying boat of World War II.** ABOVE RIGHT: **The Japanese boat was larger overall than the famed Sunderland used by the RAF.** RIGHT: **Well armed and with excellent overall performance, the H8K was a formidable opponent for Allied fighter aircraft.**

The Navy was appropriately impressed with the aircraft, but flight-testing of the H8K in late 1940 was far from uneventful, and numerous features of the aircraft had to be revised. The heavy aircraft's narrow hull, for example, caused uncontrollable porpoising in the water – when the nose lifted from the water's surface, the whole aircraft became unstable. The design team revised the hull, and production of the H8K1 (Navy Type 2 Flying Boat Model 11) began in mid-1941. Total production was a mere 175 aircraft produced in the H8K1, H8K2 (improved engines, heavier armament and radar) and 3H8K2-L (transport) versions.

The H8K was powered by four 1530hp Kasei 11s or 12s. The latter bestowed better high-altitude performance and powered late-production H8K1s. The aircraft's offensive load, carried under the inner wing, was either two 801kg/1763lb torpedoes, eight 250kg/550lb bombs, or 16 60kg/132lb bombs or depth charges.

The H8K made its combat debut on the night of March 4–5, 1942. The night-bombing raid on the island of Oahu, Hawaii, was over so great a distance that even the long-range H8K had to put down to refuel from a submarine en route. Although bad weather meant that the target was not bombed, the raid showed that the H8K was a formidable weapon of war. It was the fastest and most heavily defended flying boat of World War II, and one which Allied fighter pilots found hard to down in aerial combat.

The H8K's deep hull lent itself to the development of a transport version, the H8K2-L, with two passenger decks. The lower deck reached from the nose to some two-thirds of the fuselage, while the upper deck extended from the wing to the back of the hull. Seats or benches could accommodate from 29 passengers or 64 troops in differing levels of comfort. Armament was reduced, as was fuel-carrying capability with the removal of the hull tanks.

Kawanishi H8K2

First flight: Late 1940

Power: Four Mitsubishi 1850hp Kasei radial engines

Armament: 20mm/0.78in cannon in bow, dorsal and tail turrets and in beam blisters, plus four 7.7mm/0.303in machine-guns in cockpit, ventral and side hatches

Size: Wingspan – 38m/124ft 8in
Length – 28.13m/92ft 4in
Height – 9.15m/30ft
Wing area – 160m²/1722sq ft

Weights: Empty – 18,380kg/40,454lb
Maximum take-off – 32,500kg/71,532lb

Performance: Maximum speed – 467kph/290mph
Ceiling – 8760m/28,740ft
Range – 7180km/4460 miles
Climb – 480m/1575ft per minute

Lockheed Hudson

TOP: **The Hudson was specifically designed to meet an urgent British requirement for a coastal reconnaissance bomber, but also went on to serve the USAAF.** ABOVE: **The Hudson also served with the RAAF, RNZAF and RCAF.**

The Lockheed Hudson, the first American-built aircraft to be used operationally by the RAF during World War II, was designed to meet an urgent 1938 British requirement for a long-range maritime patrol bomber and navigation trainer. Lockheed's response, after five days and nights of frenzied work, was a militarized version of the proven Lockheed 14 Super Electra. The original Lockheed Model 10 Electra was a ten-seat civil airliner which first flew in February 1934. The larger and more powerfully engined Super Electra carried 12 passengers and first flew in July 1937. Howard Hughes made a high-profile round-the-world trip in a Super Electra, and it was this type of aircraft that took Prime Minister Chamberlain to meet Hitler in September 1938. In June 1938 the British Purchasing Commission placed an order for the Lockheed aircraft, stipulating that 200 aircraft had to be delivered by the end of December 1939. A further 50 aircraft would be bought if they could be delivered by the same date.

The Hudson was an all-metal mid-wing monoplane with an eliptical cross-section fuselage and a transparent nose for bomb-aiming. Fowler flaps were fitted to improve short-field performance. The crew normally consisted of a pilot, navigator, bomb-aimer, radio operator and gunner. Armament consisted of a bomb load of up to 454kg/1000lb (in later models) and up to seven machine-guns in nose, dorsal turret, beam and ventral hatch positions.

The first flight of a Hudson I (as a modified existing aircraft there was no need or time for a prototype) was on December 10, 1938, and the first of the RAF's aircraft arrived at Liverpool docks within two months. It may be hard to believe now, but the Hudson was considered something of a hot-rod compared to the Anson it replaced in RAF service. It climbed at 366m/1200ft per minute compared to the 220m/720ft per minute of the Anson, and had a top speed around 30 per cent greater than that of the "Annie". The Hudson Mk I began squadron service with RAF Coastal Command's No.224 Squadron in the summer of 1939, and by September No.233 Squadron was also equipped, soon followed by No.220. Shortly after war broke out, Hudsons also equipped

LEFT: **The first American-built aircraft used in action by the RAF during World War II.**
BELOW LEFT: **A Hudson of No.85 Squadron RAF.**
BELOW: **Hudsons and A-29s saw action in the Mediterranean, Pacific, Indian Ocean, Carribbean and Atlantic.**

Nos.206 and 269 Squadrons. All these aircraft flew vital maritime patrol and anti-shipping missions in defence of the UK. At peak strength, the RAF's Hudson force amounted to 17 squadrons.

The Hudson earned its spurs on October 8, 1939, when a No.224 Squadron Hudson Mk I shot down a Dornier Do18D flying boat off Jutland, the first German aircraft to be claimed by the RAF during the war. In early 1940, Hudsons began to be equipped with air-to-surface-vessel radar. Based at Aldergrove in Northern Ireland, Hudsons carried out dedicated anti-submarine patrols from August 1940. The Hudson's first victory against a U-boat occurred on August 27, 1941, when an aircraft operating out of Iceland bombed and damaged *U-570* which, following strafing attacks, surrendered. A total of 25 U-boats were put out of the war by RAF Hudsons.

Hudsons also took part in more conventional operations, with 35 participating in the RAF's second "thousand bomber" raid. The Hudsons of No.161 Squadron took part in top-secret operations delivering (and retrieving) agents, arms and other supplies into enemy territory under cover of darkness.

Total production amounted to 2584, and Hudsons were also operated by the RCAF, RAAF and RNZAF fighting in the Mediterranean, South Pacific, Indian Ocean, North Atlantic and Caribbean. China, Portugal and Brazil also purchased the

Lockheed bomber. The USAAF had 490 (as the A-29), the US Navy 20 (as the PBO-1), and a further 300 were military trainers (AT-18) in the USA. It was US Navy PBO-1s that sank the first two U-boats destroyed by US forces, and a Hudson that destroyed the first for the USAAF.

Lockheed Hudson Mk I

First flight: December 10, 1938
Power: Two Wright 1100hp GR-1820-G-102A radial piston engines
Armament: Two forward-firing 7.7mm/0.303in machine-guns, plus two others in dorsal turret; up to 635kg/1400lb bomb load
Size: Wingspan – 19.96m/65ft 6in
Length – 13.51m/44ft 4in
Height – 3.61m/11ft 10in
Wing area – 51.19m²/551sq ft
Weights: Empty – 5280kg/11630lb
Maximum take-off – 7945kg/17,500lb
Performance: Maximum speed – 396kph/246mph
Ceiling – 7625m/25,000ft
Range – 3154km/1960 miles
Climb – 3048m/10,000ft in 6 minutes, 18 seconds

Martin bomber series

The Martin Model 123 was designed and built as a private venture by the Glenn L. Martin Company of Baltimore, Maryland. The aircraft, which first flew in January 1932, was hugely influential because it broke with many design traditions and set new standards for US military combat types – it was the USAAC's first all-metal monoplane bomber.

The Model 123 was a mid-wing, all-metal monoplane, and the monocoque fuselage had corrugated top and bottom surfaces. The fuselage was sufficiently deep to allow the carriage of bombs in an internal bomb bay, as opposed to the external racks of many bombers in service at the time. The main landing gear retracted backwards to be semi-recessed into the rear of the engine nacelles. In this version, three of the crew of four sat in separate open cockpits atop the fuselage.

The US Army were interested in Martin's new "hot ship", and under the designation XB-907 the aircraft was extensively tested at Wright Field. Its speed of 317kph/197mph was ahead of all the fighters in USAAC service at the time.

The aircraft was returned to Martin for modifications, including the addition of a front gun turret in place of the far-from-popular open gun position in the nose.

However, the pilot's cockpit and the dorsal gunner positions remained open to the elements. The designation was changed to XB-907A when it was returned to the Army for more tests, then in January 1933 the Army ordered 48 production versions with enclosed cockpits, designated YB-10.

The type entered squadron service in June 1934. The major production version was the B-10B powered by 775hp Wright R-1820-33s, and production B-10B deliveries began in December 1935.

The B-12 was the same as the B-10 but was powered by Pratt & Whitney engines and had the ability to carry an auxiliary fuel tank in the bomb bay.

The B-10s and derivatives remained in service with US Army bombardment squadrons until aircraft like the B-17 were available in the late 1930s, by which time it was obsolete. No US Army B-10s participated in any combat during World War II, but export aircraft (Model 139) supplied to the Netherlands saw action against the Japanese in 1942. Other export customers were Argentina, China, the Soviet Union, Siam and Turkey. The sole remaining Martin B-10 is preserved by the United States Air Force Museum.

TOP AND ABOVE: **An advanced US bomber for the time, the B-10 served until being replaced by the next generation of bombers like the B-17. Dutch and Chinese examples were used for missions against the Japanese. Although the type was outmoded by then, it still enjoyed some successful missions. The aircraft pictured above is preserved by the United States Air Force Museum.**

Martin B-10B

First flight: January 1932 (Model 123)

Power: Two Wright 775hp R-1820-33 Cyclone radial piston engines

Armament: Three 7.62mm/0.3in machine-guns in nose and rear turrets and in ventral position; up to 1026kg/2260lb bomb load

Size: Wingspan – 21.49m/70ft 6in
Length – 13.64m/44ft 9in
Height – 4.7m/15ft 5in
Wing area – 62.99m²/678sq ft

Weights: Empty – 4395kg/9681lb
Maximum take-off – 7445kg/16,400lb

Performance: Maximum speed – 343kph/213mph
Ceiling – 7381m/24,200ft
Range – 1996km/1240 miles
Climb – 567m/1860ft per minute

LEFT: **Few Marylands remained in Britain, and the type became the first US-supplied bomber used by the RAF in North Africa.**

Martin Maryland

The Martin 167 Maryland was built to a USAAC specification, but the type was only operated by France and Britain. It was designed for both reconnaissance and bombing, and four squadrons of the French Air Force were equipped with the type at the time of the German invasion in May 1940.

Britain ordered its own Marylands and took delivery of diverted French orders after France fell. This required all the considerable labelling in the aircraft to be changed from French to English. These early aircraft were designated Maryland Is in RAF service and were followed by the more powerfully engined Maryland IIs. A total of 225 aircraft served with the Royal Air Force and virtually all served in the Middle East.

Martin Maryland Mk II

First flight: March 14, 1939
Power: Two Pratt & Whitney 1200hp R-1830-S3C4G Twin Wasp radial piston engines
Armament: Four 7.7mm/0.303in wing-mounted machine-guns, plus two more in dorsal and ventral positions; up to 908kg/2000lb bomb load
Size: Wingspan – 18.69m/61ft 4in
Length – 14.22m/46ft 8in
Height – 4.57m/14ft 11.75in
Wing area – 50.03m²/538.5sq ft
Weights: Empty – 5090kg/11,213lb
Maximum take-off – 7631kg/16,809lb
Performance: Maximum speed – 447kph/278mph
Ceiling – 7930m/26,000ft
Range – 1947km/1210 miles
Climb – 546m/1790ft per minute

Malta-based Marylands provided valuable reconnaissance cover in the region, and those of the Desert Air Force's Nos.39 and 223 Squadrons were effective light bombers. The type also equipped four South African Air Force squadrons active in the Western Desert.

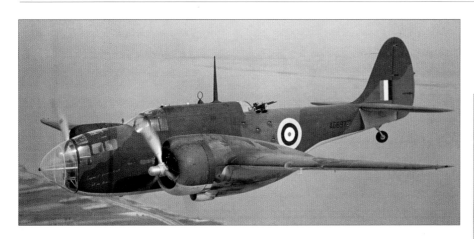

LEFT: **A Baltimore I in flight. Of the RAF's first batch of 400 aircraft, 41 were lost at sea in transit.**

Martin Baltimore

Martin Baltimore Mk IV

First flight: June 14, 1941
Power: Two Wright 1660hp R-2600-19 Cyclone 14 radial piston engines
Armament: Four 7.7mm/0.303in wing-mounted machine-guns, two or four more in dorsal turret, two 7.63mm/0.3in in ventral position; up to 908kg/2000lb bomb load
Size: Wingspan – 18.69m/61ft 4in
Length – 14.8m/48ft 5.75in
Height – 5.41m/17ft 9in
Wing area – 50.03m²/538.5sq ft
Weights: Empty – 7018kg/15,460lb
Maximum take-off – 10,260kg/22,600lb
Performance: Maximum speed – 491kph/305mph
Ceiling – 7106m/23,300ft
Range – 1530km/950 miles
Climb – 4572m/15,000ft in 12 minutes

Unlike the Maryland, the Baltimore was designed specifically to meet Royal Air Force requirements. Although it was developed from the Maryland and had the same wing, the Baltimore had more powerful engines and, most apparently, a deeper fuselage to allow better communication between the crew. Despite this, the narrow fuselage made movement around the aircraft in an emergency almost impossible. The RAF ordered 400 in May 1940 but 1575 were ultimately produced for them. They were used solely in the Mediterranean, the first joining No.223 Squadron.

The crew of four consisted of a pilot, navigator/bomb-aimer, top gunner and a radio operator who also manned the ventral gun position. Baltimore Marks I to IV had 1600hp Wright GR-2600-A5B radial engines, while the V and VI had the upgraded 1700hp Wright engines.

Desert Air Force Baltimores flew day and night bombing missions in support of ground troops in the North African campaign. Later, the type was used for intensive bombing ahead of invading Allied troops in Italy.

Martin Mariner

Martin had a history of producing flying boats, and in 1937 the company began work on a design to replace the Consolidated Catalina in US Navy service. Martin's Model 162, naval designation XPBM-1 (Experimental Patrol Bomber Martin 1), had a deep hull and shoulder-mounted gull wings, a flat twin-fin tail and inward-retracting wing floats. The gull wing design was used to produce the greatest possible distance between the engines and sea water. A less than half-scale single-seat version was produced to test the aerodynamics of the design, and its success led to the first flight of the full-scale prototype XPBM-1 in 1939.

The XPBM-1 prototype first flew in February 1939 and test-flights called for a redesign of the tail, which resulted in the dihedral configuration that matched the angle of the main wings. The aircraft had been ordered before the test-flight, so the first production model, the PBM-1, appeared quite quickly in October 1940 with service deliveries being complete by April 1941. By now the type was named Mariner. The PBM-1 had a crew of seven and was armed with five 12.7mm/0.5in Browning machine-guns. One gun was mounted in a flexible position in the tail, one was fitted in a flexible mount on each side of the rear fuselage, another was fitted in a rear dorsal turret and one was fitted in a nose turret. In addition, the PBM-1 could carry up to 908kg/2000lb of bombs or depth charges in bomb bays that were, unusually, fitted in the engine nacelles. The doors of the bomb bays looked like those of landing gear, but the Mariner was not amphibian at this stage.

In late 1940 the US Navy ordered 379 improved Model 162Bs or PBM-3s, although around twice that number were actually produced. This order alone required the

TOP: **A PBM-1 Mariner in flight, with power provided by two Wright R-2600-6 Double Cyclones.** ABOVE: **A Mariner being serviced in the Iwo Jima area, World War II. The PBMs were the eyes of the US fleet since landplanes based in the Marianas did not have the range for the required ocean patrol coverage.**

US government-aided construction of a new Martin plant in Maryland. The -3 differed from the -1 mainly by the use of uprated Pratt & Whitney 1700hp R-2600-12 engines, larger fixed wing floats and larger bomb bays housed in enlarged nacelles. Nose and dorsal turrets were powered on this version. Early PBM-3s had three-bladed propellers, but production soon included four-bladed propellers.

The PBM-3C, rolled out in late 1942, was the next major version, with 274 built. It had better armour protection for the crew, twin gun front and dorsal turrets, an improved tail turret still with a single gun, and air-to-surface-vessel radar. In addition, many PBM-3Cs were fitted with an underwing searchlight in the field.

US Navy Mariners saw extensive use in the Pacific, guarding the Atlantic western approaches and defending the Panama Canal. It was concluded that most Mariners were not likely to encounter fighter opposition, so much of the defensive armament was deleted – once the guns, turrets

LEFT: **A Mariner being prepared for hoisting by a US Navy seaplane tender, believed to be at the time of the Korean War.** BELOW: **US Navy Mariners flying over the Brazilian capital of Rio de Janeiro as they escorted an Allied convoy into port.** BOTTOM LEFT: **The pilot of a US Navy PBM-3S starts his port engine as crewmen stand by in case of fire at a Caribbean naval air station, 1944. The large protuberance above the cockpit area is a powerful anti-submarine search radar.**

and ammunition were removed, the weight saving resulted in a 25 per cent increase in the range of the lighter PBM-3S anti-submarine version. However, the nose guns were retained for offensive fire against U-boats and other surface targets. Despite this development, a more heavily armed and armoured version, the PBM-3D, was produced by re-engining some 3Cs. Larger non-retractable floats and self-sealing fuel tanks were also a feature of this version.

Deliveries of the more powerfully engined PBM-5 began in August 1944, and 589 were delivered before production ceased at the end of the war. With the PBM-5A amphibian version (of which 40 were built), the Mariner finally acquired a tricycle landing gear. The Mariner continued to serve with the US Navy and US Coast Guard into the early 1950s, and over 500 were in service at the time of the Korean War. The USCG retired its last Mariner in 1958.

Martin PBM-3D Mariner

First flight: February 18, 1939 (XPBM-1)
Power: Two Wright 1900hp R-2600-22 Cyclone radial piston engines
Armament: Eight 12.7mm/0.5in machine-guns in nose, dorsal, waist and tail positions; up to 3632kg/8000lb of bombs or depth charges
Size: Wingspan – 35.97m/118ft
　　　Length – 24.33m/79ft 10in
　　　Height – 8.38m/27ft 6in
　　　Wing area – 130.8m²/1408sq ft
Weights: Empty – 15,061kg/33,175lb
　　　Maximum take-off – 26,332kg/58,000lb
Performance: Maximum speed – 340kph/211mph
　　　Ceiling – 6035m/19,800ft
　　　Range – 3605km/2240 miles
　　　Climb – 244m/800ft per minute

Martin B-26 Marauder

In 1939 the US Army Air Corps issued a demanding specification for a high-speed medium bomber, and Martin's Model 179 proposal was so impressive that the aircraft was ordered into production off the drawing board. The aircraft was a shoulder-wing monoplane with a spacious circular cross-section fuselage for a crew of five and a retractable tricycle landing gear for improved visibility on the ground.

The first aircraft flew on November 25, 1940, and the first B-26s went to the 22nd Bomb Group at Langley Field, Virginia. This was quite a transition because the B-26 weighed two and a half times as much as the B-18 it was replacing, and had a landing speed that was 50 per cent greater. Although the original specification was exceeded, the aircraft did exhibit difficult low-speed handling, which led to an early high accident rate. Modifications improved low-speed performance and revisions to training overcame the problem, and on December 8, 1941, the day after the Japanese attack on Pearl Harbor, the USA deployed B-26s to Australia.

The first B-26 mission flown was by the 22nd Bomb Group on April 5, 1942. Taking off from Garbutt Field, Australia, the aircraft first staged through an airfield near Port Moresby, New Guinea, before attacking the Japanese base at Rabaul in New Britain.

The A-model carried more fuel, heavier armament and could carry a torpedo for maritime attack. On June 4, 1942, during the Battle of Midway, four Marauders set off to carry out the type's first torpedo attack in action against Japanese

ABOVE: **In May 1943, the B-26 became the principal medium bomber of the US Ninth Air Force in Europe. The aircraft pictured here was restored to flying condition, and appears at US air shows.**

carriers. The torpedo runs began at 244m/800ft, the aircraft then dropping down to around 3m/10ft above the sea while under heavy attack from Japanese fighters. Two B-26s were lost in the attack, the other two were seriously damaged and none of the torpedoes found their mark. The conclusion drawn from this rare tragic chapter in B-26 history was that the type was simply unsuited to this form of attack.

By November 1942 the B-26Bs (with bigger engines, more armour and, in later aircraft, bigger wings) and B-26Cs (B-models produced in Nebraska) began to see action in North Africa with 12 units of the US 12th Air Force. These aircraft, operating in a tactical bomber role, supported Allied ground forces as they fought through Corsica, Italy, Sardinia, Sicily and then southern France.

B-26s of the US Ninth Air Force, initially based in Britain in support of the D-Day landings, ranged over northern Europe attacking airfields, roads, bridges, railroads and V-1 flying bomb facilities. Despite early safety issues, the Marauder went on to have the lowest attrition rate per sortie of any American aircraft operated by the US Air Forces in Europe.

Under Lend-Lease, the Royal Air Force ordered a total of 522 Marauders and deployed them all, like the Martin Maryland and Baltimore before them, only in the Mediterranean theatre

RIGHT: **Because the B-26 was ordered straight from the drawing-board, there were no prototypes, but most of the first batch of 201 were retained for testing and training. The aircraft shown here is a JM-1, a US Navy/Marine Corps target tug/trainer version of the B-26B.**

and with the South African Air Force. No.14 Squadron was the first RAF unit to be equipped in August 1942, and was operational within two months. RAF B-26s also supported Allied forces in Sicily, Sardinia and Italy, and by the end of March 1944 had dropped a total of 18,288 tonnes/18,000 tons of bombs. In March 1943 six squadrons of Free French Air Force Marauders became operational. Flying alongside other Allied B-26s, the French Marauders supported the Allied invasion of southern France in August 1944.

By the end of the war, the B-26 had flown 129,943 operational sorties in the European and Mediterranean theatres alone, dropping 172,092 tonnes/169,382 tons of bombs in the process and destroying 402 enemy aircraft.

ABOVE: **Unit cost for the B-26 was 261,000 US dollars when it first entered service. This was reduced to 192,000 US dollars by 1944 owing to the numbers in production and refinement of the production lines.** LEFT: **Deliveries to the air force began in 1941, and the type was deployed to Australia the day after Pearl Harbor to combat any further Japanese aggression.**

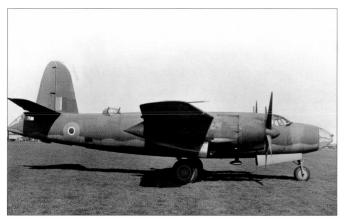

ABOVE: **The Marauder I in RAF service was equivalent to the B-26A, and had a shorter wing than later models.**

Martin B-26B Marauder 🇺🇸

First flight: November 25, 1940
Power: Two Pratt & Whitney 1920hp R-2800-43 radial piston engines
Armament: 12.7mm/0.5in machine-guns in nose, tail, top turret and fixed forward-firing on side of fuselage
Size: Wingspan – 21.64m/71ft
Length – 17.75m/58ft 3in
Height – 6.55m/21ft 6in
Wing area – 61.13m²/658sq ft
Weights: Empty – 10,896kg/24,000lb
Maximum take-off –16,798kg/37,000lb
Performance: Maximum speed – 454kph/282mph
Ceiling – 6405m/21,000ft
Range – 1851km/1150 miles
Climb – 4572m/15,000ft in 13 minutes

Mitsubishi G4M

The G4M, codenamed "Betty" by the Allies, was the Japanese Navy's principal heavy bomber of World War I. It was designed to an extremely exacting 1937 Imperial Japanese Navy specification for a land-based bomber capable of carrying a full bomb load over 3704km/2000 nautical miles. The performance was hard to achieve and came largely at the cost of protection of the crew (in terms of armour and defensive armament) and the aircraft's fuel tanks, which were contained in the aircraft wing but without armour or the ability to self-seal when damaged.

Nicknames such as "One-Shot Lighter" and the "Flying Cigar" were coined on both sides, reflecting the aircraft's tendency to explode in flames when hit in combat – the aircraft was not popular with its crews.

The prototype first flew in October 1939 and, being a basically sound design, the type progressed through flight-testing with production beginning in late 1940. The type, now designated Navy Type 1 Attack Bomber Model 11, began to reach front-line units in the summer of 1941. The next

production version, the G4M1 Model 12, was powered by the Kasei 15 engine, which provided better performance at altitude. Late 1942 saw the appearance of the improved GM42 Model 22 with a new laminar-flow wing, larger tailplane and power provided by 1800hp Mitsubishi Kasei 21 engines.

Perhaps the type's most famous action took place on December 10, 1941, three days after the attack on Pearl Harbor. G4Ms and G3Ms of the 22nd Air Flotilla sank two British capital ships, the *Prince of Wales* and the *Repulse*, off the coast of Malaya. The two ships were the first capital ships ever to be sunk by air attack at sea while free to evade. In March 1942, G4Ms made the first bombing attacks on the port of Darwin in northern Australia.

A number of earlier models were designated G4M2e Model 24J when modified to carry the MXY-7 Okha piloted kamikaze missile. Due to the great weight increase, the G4M2e was very

RIGHT: **In service from mid-1943, the G4M2 was a refined version of the Japanese bomber but lacked the range of the earlier versions.**
BELOW: **G4M1s – the original version of Japan's numerically most important bomber, in service throughout the Pacific war.**

Mitsubishi G4M3 Model 34

First flight: October 23, 1939

Power: Two Mitsubishi MK4T Kasei 25 radial engines

Armament: Four 20mm/0.78in cannon and two 7.7mm/0.303in machine-guns; up to 1000kg/2201lb of bombs or one 800kg/ 1761lb torpedo

Size: Wingspan – 25m/82ft 0.25in
Length – 19.5m/63ft 11.75in
Height – 6m/19ft 8.25in
Wing area – 78.13m²/840sq ft

Weights: Empty – 8350kg/18,378lb
Maximum take-off – 12,500kg/27,512lb

Performance: Maximum speed – 470kph/ 292mph
Ceiling – 9220m/30,250ft
Range – 4335km/2694 miles
Climb – 420m/1380ft per minute

ABOVE: **In the G4M3, the designers remedied the earlier versions' tendency to ignite so readily when hit in combat.** RIGHT: **The great range of the earlier G4Ms was only achieved at the expense of protective armour for the crew.** BELOW: **This "Betty", pictured near Singapore, was captured by the RAF in Malaya. In addition to RAF roundels, the aircraft bears the letters ATAIU SEA for Allied Technical Air Intelligence Unit, South-east Asia. The aircraft is being evaluated but flown by Japanese naval pilots under the close armed supervision of RAF officers.**

slow when carrying the weapon, and the combination had a disastrous combat debut on March 21, 1945, when most were shot down by carrier-based Allied fighter aircraft before they could launch their missiles.

Long range was not a prime concern once the Allies began to force their way towards Japan itself, and in the G4M3 Model 34, which first flew in early 1944, self-sealing fuel tanks and protective armour for the crew were introduced. Only 60 had been built by the end of the war.

In August 1942, Rabaul-based G4Ms flew the first counter-attacks against US forces invading Guadalcanal. Of 26 aircraft in the attack, at least 17 were shot down in a single raid. One aircraft damaged by ground fire made a suicide attack on the

transport ship *George F. Elliott*. G4Ms operated throughout the six-month battle for Guadalcanal and suffered heavy losses.

By early 1943, the Japanese Navy had developed new techniques using "Betties" for night torpedo attack. On the night of January 29–30, 1943, during the Battle of Rennell Island, G4Ms successfully torpedoed and sank the heavy cruiser *Chicago*, and in February 1944 a Betty torpedoed the US carrier *Intrepid*. On August 19, 1945 it was two G4M1s that carried the Imperial Japanese delegation to discuss the final requirements for Japan's surrender with the Allies.

Mitsubishi built a total of 2416 G4Ms, including prototypes, in addition to 30 G6M1 escort fighter versions manned by crews of ten who had no fewer than 19 guns at their disposal.

North American B-25 Mitchell

TOP: **The B-25 made its combat debut in early 1942, and the type remained in the front line throughout World War II.** ABOVE: **FV914, an RAF Mitchell II (B-25D) looses its bomb load. The Mk II was the main version of around 800 examples operated by the RAF.**

In the late 1930s, the US Army was looking for an "Aircraft-Bombardment Type-Medium" to fill the gap in its inventory between its light and heavy bombers. North American's response was the NA-40, which developed into the B-25 Mitchell, one of the most widely used aircraft of World War II. The B-25 entered USAAF service in 1941 and was in action until the end of the war, but the type will forever be known as the aircraft that carried out the April 1942 Doolittle raid against Tokyo from the carrier USS *Hornet*. However, the first action of a B-25 was probably the sinking of a Japanese submarine on Christmas Eve 1941. The Mitchell was named after Colonel "Billy" Mitchell who was court-martialled in the 1920s for his far-sighted views on US air power and strategic bombing.

Early production versions were eclipsed by the much-redesigned B-25C/D, which was the same aircraft built at different locations – C-models were built by North American at Inglewood while Ds were produced at NA's Dallas plant. In total some 3909 examples of the C/D were built, and 533 were supplied to the Royal Air Force as Mitchell IIs. Under the Lend-Lease deal between Britain and the USA, the RAF acquired a total of over 800 examples of this robust and reliable bomber. The B-25 first entered RAF service with Nos.98 and 180 Squadrons in September 1942, and from August 1943 they operated as part of the Second Tactical Air Force, carrying out pre-D-Day attacks on targets in Northern France as well as on V-1 "doodlebug" sites in the Pas de Calais. A total of 870 C/Ds were also supplied to the Soviet Union.

The next production variant was the B-25G, which was developed from a C-model modified to carry a US Army 75mm/2.93in field gun in the nose. This seemingly far-fetched proposal resulted in the production of 405 examples which

North American B-25H Mitchell

First flight: August 19, 1940 (production B-25)

Power: Two Wright 1700hp R-2600-13 radial piston engines

Armament: One 75mm/2.93in cannon, fourteen 12.7mm/0.5in machine-guns; up to 1362kg/ 3000lb bomb load or one 908kg/2000lb torpedo, plus up to eight rocket projectiles

Size: Wingspan – 20.6m/67ft 7in

Length – 15.54m/51ft

Height – 4.8m/15ft 9in

Wing area – 56.67 m²/610sq ft

Weights: Empty – 9068kg/19,975lb

Maximum take-off – 16,365kg/36,047lb

Performance: Maximum speed – 442kph/275mph

Service ceiling – 7259m/23,800ft

Range – 4344km/2700 miles

Climb – 4572m/15,000ft in 19 minutes

ABOVE: **The Doolittle raid is the best-known B-25 mission, but the bomber carried out countless vital missions while serving with the USAAF, USN, USMC and RAF.** RIGHT: **The heavily armed B-25J was produced in greater numbers than any other version.**

carried 21 6.81kg/15lb shells for use against ground targets and shipping. The improved B-25H carried a lighter 75mm/2.93in gun but also had four 12.7mm/0.5in guns in the nose, a further four in blisters on the sides of the nose, two more in a dorsal turret and in the tail, two in the waist positions, as well as a bomb load of 1362kg/3000lb and up to eight rocket projectiles fired from beneath the wings. One thousand examples of this hard-hitting B-25 version were built, and they saw extensive service in the Pacific.

The most numerous version of all was the B-25J, with more than 4300 examples delivered before the end of the war. This example lost the 75mm/2.93in gun but retained the other armament of the H-model. This version saw action in the Pacific, the Mediterranean and in South-east Asia. In RAF service this version was known as the Mitchell III.

The B-25 was one of the most widely used aircraft of World War II, serving with the United States Army Air Forces, Navy and Marine Corps, and was supplied to the USSR, Britain, China, Australia, Canada, France and the Netherlands.

In January 1943, B-25s were ordered by the US Navy for the US Marine Corps. Their 706 B-25s (C,D, H and J-models) were designated PBJs, and supported marine landings during the island-hopping campaigns of the drive to the Japanese home islands.

Post-war, in addition to equipping smaller air forces, many B-25s were used as training and light transport aircraft. The last B-25 in US military service was a VIP transport retired on May 21, 1960. The aircraft's stability and ease of adaptation led a number to be used as camera ships for the film industry, and some fly on in this role today.

ABOVE: **The B-25 was widely operated post-war, and a number of B-25s are preserved by collectors and museums.**

Short Stirling

The Short S.29 Stirling was one of 11 designs proposed by numerous aircraft manufacturers to satisfy the Air Ministry Specification B12/36. This called for a four-engined heavy bomber that could carry a bomb load of 6356kg/ 14,000lb over a distance of 4827km/3000 miles. The wingspan of the new bomber was not to exceed 30.5m/100ft so that the aircraft could comfortably pass through the doors of most Royal Air Force hangars of the time. It was this limitation that really defined much of the Stirling's operating parameters. The wings did not have the lifting ability to carry a fully laden Stirling to the ideal higher altitudes, but at low altitude, the aircraft was the fastest of the RAF's heavies.

The Stirling was Short's first aircraft with a retractable undercarriage, as the company was more used to producing flying boats with hulls and floats. To test the soundness of their design Shorts first produced a half-scale prototype, which flew in September 1938. In testing, it was decided to increase the length of the undercarriage legs to increase the wing's angle of attack, which would in turn reduce take-off and landing runs. The solution was not without problems – the large and complex undercarriage led to a number of accidents in service. In addition, production Stirlings stood over 7m/nearly 23ft high as a result. It is worth noting that unlike the Lancaster (derived from the twin-engine Manchester) and the Halifax (originally to be powered by two Vulture engines), the Stirling was designed from the outset as a four-engined machine.

TOP: **The Stirling III was the standard RAF bomber version from 1943.**

ABOVE: **The long undercarriage legs of the Stirling are clear in this photograph – the ground crew are dwarfed by the machine.**

The Stirling was the first of the RAF's new four-engined bombers to fly, the full-size prototype first taking to the air in May 1939. At the end of the maiden flight, a brake locked on landing and the resulting crash wrote off the aircraft. The second prototype's first flight was almost as eventful when an engine failed on take-off. Despite these shaky beginnings, the Stirling reached front-line units in August 1940 when No.7 Squadron at RAF Leeming took delivery of the new heavy bomber. The type made its combat debut, again with No.7 then based at Oakington, on the night of February 10–11, 1941, when three aircraft dropped 56 227kg/500lb bombs on oil storage tanks near Rotterdam. RAF Stirlings attacked Berlin for the first time in April 1941 and the type participated in all the 1942 thousand-bomber raids.

Some shortcomings of the original design were addressed in the Mark III, powered by Hercules XVI engines, which became the standard Bomber Command version in 1943–4. However, by mid-1943 the Stirling was sustaining higher losses than other heavies, and one source states that within five months of being introduced, 67 out of 84 aircraft delivered were lost to enemy action or written off after crashes. During the year, the Stirlings were gradually phased out of the RAF's main bomber force and moved to attacks on less well-defended targets and less dangerous duties such as mine-laying. The Stirling's final Bomber Command operation was flown by No.149 Squadron against Le Havre on September 8, 1944.

However by mid-1944 the Stirlings had found a new lease of life as troop-carriers and glider-tugs, and they performed great service on D-Day. RAF Stirling units in action on D-Day were Fairford-based Nos.90 and 622, and from Keevil Nos.196 and 299 Squadrons.

As the Allies fought their way through Europe after D-Day, Stirlings were also used in support of the RAF's Second Tactical Air Force transporting 120 22.7 litre/5 gallon jerry cans full of petrol at a time. In addition to glider-tug duties, the Stirling was used to drop food supplies and ammunition to the French resistance, and also to drop airborne troops.

Post-war, a number of Stirling Vs (a dedicated transport version built for RAF Transport Command) were used as passenger aircraft between England and the continent for a brief time.

RIGHT: **Stirlings of No.7 Squadron, probably at Oakington in Cambridgeshire.**
BELOW: **Two Stirlings of No.7 Squadron fly across the flat open spaces of East Anglia.**

ABOVE: **The Stirling was a large aircraft but due to its construction, the largest bomb it could carry was 1816kg/4000lb. Here, an armourer prepares a "cookie" bomb prior to loading it aboard the waiting aircraft.**

Short Stirling Mk III

First flight: May 14, 1939 (full-size prototype)
Power: Bristol 1650hp Hercules XVI radial engines
Armament: Eight 7.7mm/0.303in machine-guns in nose, dorsal and tail turrets; up to 6356kg/14,000lb bomb load
Size: Wingspan – 30.2m/99ft 1in
  Length – 26.59m/87ft 3in
  Height – 6.93m/22ft 9in
  Wing area – 135.63m²/1460sq ft
Weights: Empty – 19,613kg/43,200lb
  Maximum take-off – 31,780kg/70,000lb
Performance: Maximum speed – 435kph/270mph
  Ceiling – 5185m/17,000ft
  Range – 950km/590 miles with full bomb load
  Climb – 244m/800ft per minute

Short Sunderland

The Sunderland is a rare type of military aeroplane – one that was derived from a civil aircraft. Based upon the Short C Class "Empire" flying boats operated by Imperial Airways in the 1930s, the Short "Sunderland" became one of the Royal Air Force's longest serving operational aircraft over the next two decades. One of the finest flying boats ever built, during World War II the Sunderland played a decisive role in the defeat of German U-boats in the Battle of the Atlantic.

Although the first flight of the prototype Sunderland took place in October 1937, the Air Ministry was already familiar with the aircraft's successful civilian counterpart, and had placed an order in March the preceding year.

In early June 1938 the first batch of production Sunderland Mk Is were delivered to No.230 Squadron based in Singapore. The Sunderland replaced the RAF's mixed fleet of biplane flying boats and represented a huge leap in capability.

By the outbreak of World War II in September 1939, three Coastal Command squadrons had become operational and were ready to seek out and destroy German U-boats. The Sunderland also became a very welcome sight to the many seamen from sunken vessels and airmen who had had to ditch their aircraft. When the British merchant ship *Kensington Court* was torpedoed 113km/70 miles off the Scillies on September 18, 1939, two patrolling Sunderlands had the entire crew of 34 back on dry land just an hour after the ship sank.

TOP: **This Sunderland was converted to "Sandringham" civilianized standard post-war, although some would say that life aboard a Sunderland was quite civilized. Few RAF combat aircraft have ever had a kitchen or, more correctly, a galley.** ABOVE: **A Mark II built by Shorts at Rochester, operated by No.10 Squadron. This Australian squadron became part of Coastal Command at the start of World War II, and operated in the Atlantic.**

The Sunderland, with its crew of ten, was heavily armed and became known to the Luftwaffe as the Flying Porcupine. Many times during the war a lone Sunderland fought off or defeated a number of attacking aircraft.

Although Sunderlands did engage in many a "shoot-out" with German vessels, sometimes the sight of the large aircraft was enough to have an enemy crew scuttle their boat – such was the case on January 31, 1940, when the arrival of an aircraft from No.228 Squadron prompted the crew of U-Boat *U-55* to do just that.

At the end of 1940 the Mk II was introduced, with four Pegasus XVIII engines with two-stage superchargers, a twin-gun dorsal turret, an improved rear turret and ASV (air-to-surface-vessel) Mk II radar. The most numerous version was the Mk III that first flew in December 1941. This variant had a modified hull for improved planing when taking off. This was

LEFT: **This Sunderland III, W3999, was the first production machine of the version, and had its maiden flight on December 15, 1941. The III had a dorsal gun turret as standard, as well as a refined hull.** BELOW LEFT: **A Sunderland V of No.230 Squadron. The Mk V entered RAF service in early 1945 and remained the standard RAF flying boat until 1959.** BELOW: **At home on water or in the air, the Sunderland's ability to find and destroy U-boats made it a key aircraft in the fight against Nazi Germany.**

followed by a larger and heavier version designated the Mk IV/ Seaford. After evaluation by the RAF, the project of the flying boat was abandoned.

The Sunderland Mk V was the final version, and made its appearance at the end of 1943. It was powered by four 1200hp Pratt & Whitney R-1830-90 Twin Wasp engines and carried ASV Mk VI radar. By the end of the final production run in 1945 a total of 739 Sunderlands had been built, and after World War II, many continued to serve with the British, French, Australian, South African and New Zealand air forces.

Post-war, RAF Sunderlands delivered nearly 5080 tonnes/ 5000 tons of supplies during the Berlin Airlift, and during the Korean War they were the only British aircraft to operate throughout the conflict. During the Malayan Emergency RAF Sunderlands carried out bombing raids on land against terrorists.

The Sunderland finally retired from the Royal Air Force on May 15, 1959, when No.205 Squadron flew the last sortie for the type from RAF Changi, Singapore, where the illustrious operational career of the Sunderland flying boat had begun 21 years earlier. However, the last air arm to retire the type from military service was the Royal New Zealand Air Force in March 1967. A total of 749 Sunderlands were built between 1937 and 1946.

Short Sunderland Mk V

First Flight: October 16, 1937 (prototype)

Power: Four Pratt & Whitney 1200hp R-1830 Twin Wasp 14-cylinder air-cooled radials

Armament: Eight 7.7mm/0.303in Browning machine-guns in turrets, four fixed 7.7mm/ 0.303in Browning machine-guns in nose, two manually operated 12.7mm/0.5in machine-guns in beam positions; 2252kg/4,960lb of depth charges or bombs

Size: Wingspan – 34.36m/112ft 9in
Length – 26m/85ft 3in
Height – 10.01m/32ft 11in
Wing area – 138.14m²/1487sq ft

Weights: Empty – 16,798kg/37,000lb
Maximum take-off – 27,240kg/60,000lb

Performance: Maximum speed – 343 kph/213mph
Ceiling – 5456m/17,900ft
Range – 4795 km/2980miles
Climb – 256m/840ft per minute

Tupolev SB

This aircraft is often incorrectly referred to as the SB-2, which is more a Western corruption of the designation SB-2-M100A meaning SB with 2xM100A engines. It was designed to a 1933 Soviet Air Force specification for a fast light bomber with a maximum level speed of 330kph/205mph, a ceiling of 8000m/26,250ft, range of 700km/434 miles and the ability to carry a 500kg/1100lb bomb load. The Tupolev ANT-40 SB (*skorostnoy bombardirovschik* or high-speed bomber) incorporated elements of earlier Tupolev designs and was of metal stressed-skin construction.

This fast, well-armed bomber first flew on April 25, 1934, with power provided by two US Wright Cyclone radials. After a landing accident it was rebuilt and re-engined with Soviet M-87 engines.

Production began in 1935, with early aircraft powered by 750hp M-100 engines and then 860hp 100As. The SB-2bis was the last production version, and first flew in October 1936 with power provided by two 960hp M-103s. Around 6650 SBs were built in total before production ended in late 1940.

SBs were supplied to the Republican forces during the Spanish Civil War. While some nations used Spain as a testing ground, providing aircraft and manpower free of charge, the Soviet Union required hard currency before allowing their aircraft to take part. SBs also saw action during the Nomonhan Incident, a border skirmish that became a small war against the Japanese in Mongolia during 1939. The type was also used against Finnish forces during the Winter War, but was beginning to show its age when faced with fast and agile fighters.

ABOVE: **The SB was built in great numbers, and was the first stressed-skin aircraft built in the Soviet Union. The radial engines were later replaced with in-line powerplants, which bestowed better performance.** BELOW LEFT: **The SB was widely used, seeing action in the Spanish Civil War, and with the Chinese Air Force against Japan. Czech machines were seized by the Luftwaffe and used as target tugs.**

At the start of Operation Barbarossa, the German invasion of the Soviet Union in June 1941, 71 out of 82 Bomber Air Regiments operated the type. Many were lost when attacked by Luftwaffe fighters when having no fighter protection of their own. The SB was one of the Soviet Air Force's primary bombers until its withdrawal began in 1943, by which time it was operating largely at night.

Czechoslovakia imported a number of SBs and then produced its own licensed version known as the B-71. Among a number of variants, Tupolev produced a civil transport, the PS-40, for Aeroflot.

Tupolev SB-2bis

First flight: April 25, 1934
Power: Two 960hp M-103 piston engines
Armament: Six 7.62mm/0.3in machine-guns; up to 600kg/1320lb bomb load
Size: Wingspan – 20.33m/66ft 8.5in
Length –12.57m/41ft 2.75in
Height – 3.25m/10ft 8in
Wing area – 56.7m²/610.33sq ft
Weights: Empty – 4768kg/10,494lb
Maximum take-off – 7880kg/17,344lb
Performance: Maximum speed – 450kph/280mph
Ceiling – 7800m/25,590ft
Range – 2300km/1429 miles
Climb – 400m/1310ft per minute

LEFT: Soviet TB-3s saw action against Finland, Japan and Poland, as well as invading German forces.

Tupolev TB-3

This large four-engined low-wing bomber was the most advanced bomber in the world for a time. It made its maiden flight on December 22, 1930, and production was underway within a year. The first service aircraft were delivered to the Soviet Air Force in early 1932.

Everything about this aircraft was big and it had a heavier maximum take-off weight than any other aircraft at the time.

The TB-3s had a corrugated metal covering similar to that used by Junkers. The wings were so thick they contained "crawl-ways" giving access to the engines during flight. The pilot and co-pilot sat side by side in an open cockpit with separate windscreens.

Continually modified, over 500 of these bombers remained in service at the time of the German invasion in 1941, and some carried out night-bombing

Tupolev TB-3 M-17

First flight: December 22, 1930
Power: Four 715hp M-17F piston engines
Armament: Eight 7.7mm/0.303in machine-guns in nose and dorsal positions, and in two retractable underwing "dustbins"; up to 2000kg/4402lb bomb load
Size: Wingspan – 39.5m/129ft 7in
　　　　Length – 24.4m/80ft 0.75in
　　　　Height – 8.2m/26ft 9in
　　　　Wing area – 230m²/2475.8sq ft
Weights: Empty – 10,967kg/24,138lb
　　　　Maximum take-off – 17,200kg/37,857lb
Performance: Maximum speed – 197kph/122mph
　　　　Ceiling – 3800m/12,470ft
　　　　Range – 1350km/839 miles
　　　　Climb – Not known

attacks against the invaders. Paratroop conversions could carry up to 35 troops in the fuselage and wings.

LEFT: Post-war, the Tu-2S served with the Polish and Chinese air forces.

Tupolev Tu-2

This potent medium bomber, initially known as the ANT-61, first entered Soviet Air Force service in 1942, and from the outset it proved to be a key weapon in the Soviet inventory. It was fast, very well armed, handled well and needed few upgrades or improvements during its service life. The Tu-2S, the second main production version, differed

from earlier examples by having uprated engines, greater bomb load and heavier gun armament.

Unlike many of its contemporaries, the Tu-2 continued to serve after World War II and saw considerable use with North Korea during the Korean War. Wartime production was around 1100 but a further 1400 were built post-war.

Tupolev Tu-2S

First flight: January 29, 1941 (prototype ANT-58)
Power: Two 1850hp Ash-82FNV radial piston engines
Armament: Two 20mm/0.78in cannon, three 12.7mm/0.5in machine-guns; up to 4000kg/8804lb bomb load
Size: Wingspan – 18.86m/61ft 10.5in
　　　　Length – 13.8m/45ft 3.5in
　　　　Height – 4.55m/14ft 11in
　　　　Wing area – 48.8m²/525.3sq ft
Weights: Empty – 7474kg/16,450lb
　　　　Maximum take-off – 11,360kg/25,003lb
Performance: Maximum speed – 550kph/342mph
　　　　Ceiling – 9500m/31,170ft
　　　　Range – 1400km/870 miles
　　　　Climb – 700m/2300ft per minute

Some Communist nations operated the type until 1961, which speaks volumes for the quality of the design of this bomber which had the NATO reporting name of "Bat".

Vickers Vimy

In 1917, the British were developing bombers capable of bombing the German heartland. Had World War I not come to an end in November 1918, these bombers, among them the Vickers Vimy, would have formed strategic bomber fleets attempting to pound Germany into submission. Although the war came to an end before the Vimy saw action, the type continued to serve in the RAF as a front-line bomber until the late 1920s.

The biplane Vimy was a large aircraft for its day with a wingspan of over 20m/68ft, and the prototype B9952 first flew on November 17, powered by two 207hp Hispano-Suiza engines. Of wooden construction and fabric-covered, the Vimy had a crew of three and could carry a bomb load in excess of a ton – this was a far cry from the hand-held bombs thrown overboard from the early World War I bombers.

Although many aircraft contracts were cancelled at the war's end, the Vimy continued to be supplied to the Royal Air Force. The main production version of the Vimy was the Mark IV powered by Rolls-Royce Eagle VIII engines, and some 240 were built – the first were delivered to the RAF in France in 1918 and the last batch were delivered to the RAF in 1925. The Vimy did not enter service fully until July 1919 when it joined No. 58 Squadron stationed in Egypt. In Britain, the first of the home squadrons to be equipped with the Vickers bomber was No.100 based at Spittlegate. No.7 Squadron was formed in June 1923 to operate Vimys, and was the Royal Air Force's UK-based heavy bomber until being augmented by the Vimys of Nos.9 and 58 Squadrons in 1924. By 1925 the Vimy

TOP: **A replica of Alcock and Brown's famous Atlantic-crossing Vimy. The Vimy's performance on that epic flight demonstrated the greatness of the design.**

ABOVE: **The Vimy was built for deep bombing missions into Germany, but some of these aircraft continued to fly in RAF service long after the end of the Great War.**

was being replaced by Vickers Virginias, but the aircraft of No.502 stationed in Northern Ireland remained in front-line service until 1929. The type was used increasingly for mail services, as a trainer and for parachute training. The Vimy design was also developed into the Vimy Commercial with an all-new large-diameter fuselage – a dedicated version was produced as the Vimy Ambulance for moving wounded personnel. The Vickers Vernon bomber-transport derivative became the first aircraft designed specifically for troop-carrying, and served mainly in Iraq in the mid- to late 1920s.

On June 14, 1919, the Vimy flew into the history books when a Vimy IV owned by the Vickers company and the thirteenth off the production line took off from Newfoundland

ABOVE AND LEFT: **Alcock and Brown's flight was an epic for its day. On their return to Britain, they became national heroes, having finally beaten the Atlantic.**

and headed eastward across the Atlantic. The two-man crew were Royal Air Force officers Captain John Alcock, who served as pilot, and Lieutenant Arthur Whitten-Brown, navigator. Also aboard the aircraft were around 3927 litres/865 gallons of highly flammable aviation fuel. For the transatlantic flight the Vimy was specially adapted – all military equipment was removed and the cockpit was widened so that the two fliers could sit side by side on a narrow wooden bench with a thin cushion for comfort. Once alterations had been made to Alcock and Brown's Vimy, the aircraft was dismantled, crated and transported to Newfoundland.

The epic, trailblazing flight, averaging 190km/118 miles per hour, was far from uneventful – the pair faced snow, ice and fog, as well as extreme tiredness. Then at 08:40 hours the next morning, after a 16-hour flight, Alcock and Brown sighted Ireland, and within minutes prepared to land. The aircraft landed in a bog and nosed over, sustaining damage, but the pioneering airmen were unhurt. As well being knighted and feted throughout their country, Alcock and Brown won the Daily Mail newspaper's prize of 10,000 pounds offered in 1913 for the first successful crossing of the Atlantic.

ABOVE: **Vimys did not reach RAF units until the end of October 1918, and then only three machines were delivered.** ABOVE LEFT: **This Vimy was built by Vickers at Bexley, and was powered by Salmson engines.**

Vickers Vimy IV

First flight: November 30, 1917
Power: Two Rolls-Royce 360hp Eagle VIII in-line piston engines
Armament: Two Lewis guns, one each in nose and mid-upper positions; 1124kg/2476lb of bombs
Size: Wingspan – 20.7m/68ft
  Length – 13.3m/44ft
  Height – 4.7m/15ft
  Wing area – 124m²/1330sq ft
Weights: Empty – 3225kg/7104lb
  Maximum take-off – 5675kg/12,500lb
Performance: Maximum speed – 166kph/103mph
  Service ceiling – 3660m/12,000ft
  Range – 1448km/900 miles
  Climb – 110m/360ft per minute

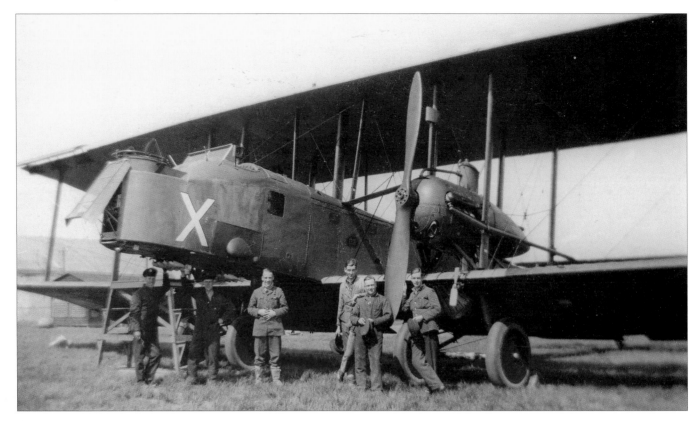

Vickers Virginia

TOP: **The Virginia was still a front-line bomber in 1937. Within seven years, the RAF was operating jet fighters.** ABOVE: **A Virginia taking part in early inflight refuelling experiments with a Westland Wapati.**

The Virginia was the standard heavy night-bomber of the Royal Air Force from 1924 until 1937, a long service in those inter-war days. Structurally it differed little from the Vimy developed by Vickers in World War I, but its performance was slightly better than its predecessor and it could carry a greater bomb load. The type was designed to meet Air Ministry specification 1/21, and first flew at Brooklands in November 1922. RAF service deliveries began in late 1924, the first recipient units being Nos.7 and 58 followed by No.9. The three squadrons took part in the famous Hendon Display in 1925, and the Virginias were popular participants at the annual show through to 1937.

The Virginia was modified considerably during its service career so that the final version in service, the X, was quite different to the early Marks. The prototype Virginia (J6856) had its Lion engines housed in rectangular nacelles, but production aircraft all featured smaller, oval-section nacelles. A total of 124 were built for the RAF in ten versions, and Marks I to V can be identified by the dihedral on the bottom wing only. The Mark VII introduced a lengthened and redesigned nose. The Mark X was the first version not to be of wooden construction, instead being all-metal with a fabric covering – this model accounted for 50 of the 124 aircraft built.

It was the Virginia that introduced the auto-pilot into RAF service, and when the type was replaced by newer bombers, it continued to serve as a parachute trainer, with jump-off platforms added to the rear of the engines. Some were still flying as engine test-beds in 1941.

ABOVE: **The roar of the Virginia's noisy Lion engines could be heard from miles away.**

Vickers Virginia Mk X

First flight: November 24, 1922
Power: Two Napier 580hp Lion VBW-12 piston engines
Armament: One 7.7mm/0.303in machine-gun in nose and two more in the tail; up to 1362kg/3000lb bomb load
Size: Wingspan – 26.72m/87ft 8in
　　　Length – 18.97m/62ft 3in
　　　Height – 5.54m/18ft 2in
　　　Wing area – 202.34m²/2178sq ft
Weights: Empty – 4381kg/9650lb
　　　Maximum take-off – 7990kg/17,600lb
Performance: Maximum speed – 174kph/108mph
　　　Ceiling – 4725m/15,500ft
　　　Range – 1585km/985 miles
　　　Climb – 152m/500ft per minute

Vickers Wellesley

The Vickers Wellesley was the first of the Vickers designs, and the first RAF aircraft to employ the unique geodetic construction developed by Barnes Wallis. Vickers had designed a biplane bomber to meet a 1931 general-purpose requirement G.4/31, and then as a private venture developed a monoplane derivative which became the Wellesley. The prototype flew on June 19, 1935, and sufficiently impressed the Air Ministry that in September an order was placed for 96 aircraft to specification 22/35, which was written around the Wellesley. As well as the unusual geodetic construction, the bomber carried innovative streamlined bomb panniers under the wings, thereby simplifying construction. In a 14-month production run which began in March 1937, a total of 176 examples were built.

The Wellesley entered RAF service in April 1937 with No.76 Squadron at Finningley, and ultimately equipped six UK-based Bomber Command squadrons. By the start of the war,

however, only four examples remained in service with Bomber Command in Britain, a hundred Wellesleys having been transferred to the Middle East. In an often overlooked episode of World War II, East Africa-based aircraft saw action against the Italians in 1940. The type also carried out maritime reconnaissance in the region until 1941.

The Wellesley is perhaps best known for its record-breaking flight undertaken in 1938 from Egypt to Australia. Three aircraft of the Long Range Development Flight set off on November 5, 1938, from Ismalia, Egypt. One had to abort en route but two Wellesleys, L2638 and L2680, flew non-stop to Darwin, Australia, covering 11,524km/7162 miles in a little over 48 hours and set a new world long-distance record. These aircraft only differed from service aircraft by having extra fuel tanks, accommodation for a third crew member and a Pegasus XXII in place of the usual XX. In service aircraft, the Mark II designation covered aircraft with a large continuous canopy over both cockpits.

TOP AND ABOVE: **The Wellesley was used in anger against Italian forces in 1940. Note the innovative bomb panniers carried beneath the aircraft's wings. The aircraft pictured here are Mk Is.**

Vickers Wellesley

First flight: June 19, 1935
Power: One Bristol 925hp Pegasus XX
Armament: One forward-firing 7.7mm/0.303in machine-gun in right wing, plus one in rear cockpit; up to 908kg/2000lb bomb load carried in underwing panniers
Size: Wingspan – 22.73m/74ft 7in
Length – 11.96m/39ft 3in
Height – 3.75m/12ft 4in
Wing area – 58.5m²/630sq ft
Weights: Empty – 2891kg/6369lb
Maximum take-off – 5039kg/11,100lb
Performance: Maximum speed – 286kph/178mph
Ceiling – 10,065m/33,000ft
Range – 4168km/2590 miles
Climb – 366m/1200ft per minute

Vickers Wellington

The Wellington was built using a unique and ingenious geodetic construction developed by the brilliant Barnes Wallis, who later developed the bouncing bomb. The aircraft's geodetic fuselage was built of a large criss-cross metal mesh which gave the aircraft incredible strength. This meant that fabric-covered Wellingtons came home with very large holes in them caused by flak or cannon fire when other aircraft would have broken up in mid-air. The "Wimpy", as the type was nicknamed (after J. Wellington Wimpy of the Popeye cartoons), first reached front-line service in October 1938 with No.99 Squadron at Mildenhall. The Wellington was the principal bomber of Bomber Command at the start of World War II with six squadrons on strength, and remained so until the four-engined heavies joined the force later in the war. On September 4, 1939, along with Blenheims, 14 Wellingtons of Nos.9 and 149 Squadrons flew the first offensive RAF bombing raid of the war against Germany.

The Wellington was Vickers' response to the British Air Ministry's 1932 specification B.9/32 for a twin-engined medium bomber. After its first flight in June 1936, the Wellington caused a stir when it made a public appearance at the annual Hendon air display later that year. The large streamlined monoplane bomber was a great advance on the biplanes that had been the norm.

The first production version to enter service was the I, which differed greatly from the prototype K4049. The fuselage shape was refined, and a retractable tailwheel was fitted together with gun turrets. The IA saw some armament changes

TOP: **This Wellington II served with No.104 Squadron RAF. The Mark II was a Mark IC, but powered by 1145hp Merlin X engines, and 400 examples were built.**
ABOVE: **The groundcrew of this Wellington had a novel means of recording the number of missions on the aircraft nose, taking inspiration from a popular beer advertisement of the period.**

but the Mark IC, of which 2685 were built, introduced beam guns instead of a ventral gun, and larger mainwheels were fitted. By mid-1941, more powerfully engined Wellington Mk IIs and Mk IIIs had entered service. As the Wellingtons flew on their daylight missions over enemy territory, the official belief was that when flying in formation the bombers would be able to defend themselves without fighter escort against marauding fighters. The reality was very different and Wellingtons, with their unsealed fuel tanks, proved to be very vulnerable. On December 18, 1939, Wellingtons of Nos.9, 37 and 149 Squadrons were sent to carry out a mission against the

LEFT: **Wellington ICs of No.311 Squadron. This photograph pre-dates the unit's transfer to Coastal Command in April 1942.** BELOW: **Wellingtons entered Coastal Command service in the spring of 1942. These Mk XIIIs had A.S.V. masts on the "spine" to search for submarines.**

ABOVE: **The end of the line – the Wellington X was the final bomber version, with over 3800 built. Post-war, many were converted to T.10 standard with a faired nose and the turret deleted.**

Schillig Roads and Wilhelmshaven. They were attacked by Luftwaffe fighters, and ten of the bombers were destroyed and three badly damaged. After this mission highlighted the aircraft's vulnerability, the Wellington was switched to night operations.

The Wellington proved to be a very successful night-bomber, and carried out bombing raids deep into Germany and Italy. The night of August 25–6, 1940 saw Wellingtons of Nos.99 and 149 Squadrons join Hampdens and Whitleys on Bomber Command's first attack on the heart of the Third Reich, Berlin. The Cologne raid of May 30, 1942 saw no fewer than 599 Wellingtons take part in the mission.

In September 1940, Wellingtons joined No.202 Group as the RAF's first long-range bombers in the Middle East. The type also saw use in the North African and Greek campaigns, and in 1942 India-based Wellingtons became the RAF's first long-range bombers operating in the Far East.

The Wellington fought on in Europe until it carried out its last offensive mission on the night of October 8–9, 1943 against Hanover. However, the "Wimpy" did continue to serve as a bomber elsewhere, and on March 13, 1945, aircraft of No.40 Squadron dropped 1816kg/4000lb "cookie" bombs on Trevisio in the Italian theatre.

Mention must also be made of the Coastal Command Wellingtons, fitted with 14.63m/48ft metal hoops that were used for exploding enemy mines in the sea below by generating a strong magnetic field. Coastal Command Wellingtons also carried out anti-submarine duties, the first enemy vessel being sunk on July 6, 1942.

Post-war, many converted Wellingtons continued to serve as training aircraft into the mid-1950s. In all 11,461 Wellingtons were built, the last of which was rolled out on October 13, 1945.

Vickers Wellington IC

First flight: June 15, 1936

Power: Two Bristol 1000hp Pegasus XVIII radial engines

Armament: Two 7.7mm/0.303in machine-guns in nose and tail turrets, two in beam positions; up to 2043kg/4500lb bomb load

Size: Wingspan – 26.26m/86ft 2in
Length – 19.68m/64ft 7in
Height – 5.31m/17ft 5in
Wing area – 78.04m²/840sq ft

Weights: Empty – 8424kg/18,556lb
Maximum take-off – 12,939kg/28,500lb

Performance: Maximum speed – 378kph/235mph
Cceiling – 5490m/18,000ft
Range – 4104km/2550 miles
Climb – 320m/1050ft per minute

Vultee Vengeance

The Vengeance was designed for the Royal Air Force, who considered that, following the combat successes of the Luftwaffe's Stuka during the Spanish Civil War and the Blitzkrieg, a dedicated purpose-designed dive-bomber should be in the RAF inventory. However, by the time the Vengeance was ready to enter service, the RAF had seen the vulnerability of the German dive-bomber through the gunsights of British fighters during the Battle of Britain. Accordingly, the RAF decided that the Vengeance was not suited to the European theatre but was appropriate for operations in the Far East and against challenging targets in Burma.

History has not been kind to the aircraft but in fact it was a very capable, stable and accurate bombing platform. In Burma, often operating out of range of friendly fighter cover, Royal Air Force and Indian Air Force Vengeances played a key role in the battles against the Japanese for Imphal and Kohima, and carried out precision bombing raids against key bridges used for moving supplies to the Japanese.

The Royal Navy's Fleet Air Arm received a total of 113 Vengeances, 88 of which had been delivered by the end of August 1945, and the rest by early 1946. No FAA aircraft saw action; they were used mainly as target tugs.

The Royal Australian Air Force took delivery of great numbers of the Vengeance from 1942, some 342 in total. The RAAF operated the type in combat in New Guinea, and after withdrawal from front-line service, the Australian aircraft flew as target tugs and communications aircraft until they

ABOVE: **Vengeance Mk III of No.84 Squadron, Burma 1944.** BELOW LEFT: **RAAF Vengeance dive-bombers of No.24 Squadron returning from a raid on Alexishafen airstrip, February 27, 1944.**

were retired in 1946. Some of the Australian machines were modified for pesticide spraying in late 1945.

The Free French Air Force operated the Vengeance in North Africa, and the aircraft was also supplied to Brazil. The USAAF commandeered some of the aircraft intended for British use but these aircraft did not see combat. By the end of production in 1944, 1528 aircraft had been built in total.

Vultee A-35B Vengeance

First flight: July 1941 (first RAF aircraft)

Power: One Wright 1700hp Double Row Cyclone R-2600 radial piston engine

Armament: Six 7.7mm/0.303in machine-guns in wings and rear cockpit; bomb load of 908kg/ 2000lb

Size: Wingspan – 14.63m/48ft
Length – 12.12 m/39ft 9in
Height – 4.67 m/15ft 4in
Wing area – 30.84sq m/332sq ft

Weights: Empty – 4676kg/10,300lb
Maximum take-off – 7445kg/16,400lb

Performance: Maximum speed – 449kph/ 279mph
Service ceiling – 6800m/22,300ft
Range – 1931km/1200 miles
Climb – 366m/1200ft per minute

Yokosuka D4Y Suisei

Yokosuka was the location for the Imperial Japanese Navy's First Naval Air Technical Arsenal, which began to design a carrier-based single-engine dive-bomber in 1938. The resulting Suisei (comet), based on the Heinkel He118, was unusual as it was one of few Japanese combat types to be powered by a liquid-cooled engine, in this case a licence-built copy of the German DB 601.

In service from autumn 1942, the type served initially in the reconnaissance role (D4Y1-C), with the dedicated dive-bomber version (D4Y1) entering service in 1943. The type did not fare well against high-performance Allied fighters, and many fell to their guns due to poor protection for the crew and the lack of self-sealing fuel tanks. A total of 2038 were built, the D4Y2 having a more

Yokosuka D4Y2	

First flight: November 1940
Power: One Aichi 1400hp Atsuta 32 piston engine
Armament: Two 7.7mm/0.303in forward-firing and one 7.92mm/0.31in rear-firing machine-gun; up to 800kg/1761lb bomb load
Size: Wingspan – 11.5m/37ft 8.75in
  Length – 10.22m/33ft 6.25in
  Height – 3.74m/12ft 3.25in
  Wing area – 23.6m²/254sq ft
Weights: Empty – 2440kg/5370lb
  Maximum take-off – 4250kg/9354lb
Performance: Maximum speed – 550kph/342mph
  Ceiling – 10,700m/35,105ft
  Range – 1465km/910 miles
  Climb – 820m/2700ft per minute

powerful engine while the D4Y4 was a kamikaze suicide-bomber version which carried one 800kg/1761lb bomb. The Allied codename allocated to all versions was "Judy".

Yokosuka P1Y1

This aircraft was built to a 1940 Imperial Japanese Navy requirement for a fast, low-flying medium bomber with the ability to launch torpedo attacks. The prototype P1Y flew in August 1943 and showed great potential, but problems with development delayed its entry into service until early 1945 as the Navy Bomber Ginga (Milky Way) Model II.

Over 1000 were built but this potent combat aircraft was dogged by maintenance problems that stopped the bomber, which could outrun fighters at low level, being a thorn in the Allies' side. It was a complex machine and experienced, well-trained maintenance personnel were in short supply. The aircraft's range at over 5000km/

Yokosuka P1Y1 Ginga	

First flight: Spring 1943
Power: Two Nakajima 1820hp Homare 11 radial piston engines
Armament: Two 20mm/0.78in cannon, one forward-firing, one rear-firing; up to 800kg/1760lb bomb load
Size: Wingspan – 20m/65ft 7.5in
  Length –15m/49ft 2.5in
  Height – 4.3m/14ft 1.25in
  Wing area – 55m²/592sq ft
Weights: Empty – 7265kg/15,990lb
  Maximum take-off – 13,500kg/29,713lb
Performance: Maximum speed – 547kph/340mph
  Ceiling – 9400m/30,840ft
  Range – 5370km/3337 miles
  Climb – 650m/2133ft per minute

3105 miles was very impressive, but among other roles the Ginga was used as a suicide-bomber before the end of the war in the Pacific. The Allied codename for the bomber was "Frances".

Glossary

AAF	Army Air Forces (USAAF)
Aerodynamics	study of how gases, including air, flow and how forces act upon objects moving through air
Ailerons	control surfaces at trailing edge of each wing used to make the aircraft roll
Angle of attack	angle of a wing to the oncoming airflow
ASV	air-to-surface-vessel – pertaining to this type of radar developed during World War II
ASW	anti-submarine warfare
Biplane	an aircraft with two sets of wings
Blister	a streamlined, often clear, large fairing on aircraft body housing guns or electronics
Ceiling	the maximum height at which an aircraft can operate
Dihedral	the upward angle of the wing formed where the wings connect to the fuselage
Dorsal	pertaining to the upper side of an aircraft
Drag	the force that resists the motion of the aircraft through the air
ECM	electronic countermeasures
Elevators	control surfaces on the horizontal part of the tail, used to alter the aircraft's pitch
ESHP	equivalent shaft horsepower
Fin	the vertical portion of the tail
Flaps	movable parts of the trailing edge of a wing used to increase lift at slower air speeds
HP	horsepower
Jet engine	an engine that works by creating a high velocity jet of air to propel it forward
Leading edge	the front edge of a wing or tailplane
Monoplane	an aircraft with one set of wings
OCU	Operational Conversion Unit (RAF)
Pitch	rotational motion in which an aircraft turns around its lateral axis
Port	left side when looking forward
Radome	protective covering for radar made from material through which radar beams can pass
RAAF	Royal Australian Air Force
RAF	Royal Air Force
RATO	rocket-assisted take-off
RCAF	Royal Canadian Air Force
RFC	Royal Flying Corps
RNAS	Royal Naval Air Service
RNZAF	Royal New Zealand Air Force
Roll	rotational motion in which an aircraft turns around its longitudinal axis
Rudder	the parts of the tail surfaces that control an aircraft's yaw (its left and right turning)
Starboard	right side when looking forward
Tailplane	horizontal part of the tail, known as horizontal stabilizer in North America
Thrust	force produced by engine which pushes an aircraft forward
USAAC	United States Army Air Corps
USAAF	United States Army Air Forces
USAF	United States Air Force
USN	United States Navy

Index

A

A-20 Boston/Havoc, Douglas, 45, 62–3
A-26/B-26 Invader, Douglas, 64–5
Aichi D3A, 30
Amiens, de Havilland/ Airco DH10, 54–5
Amiot 143, 30
Anson, Avro, 15, 34
Arado Ar 234 Blitz, 15, 31
Armstrong Whitworth Whitley, 32–3, 34, 81, 123
atomic bomb, 26–7, 41
Avenger, Grumman, 15, 76–7
Avro
    504, 11
    Anson, 15, 34
    Lancaster, 15, 20–1, 36–7, 78, 79
    Manchester, 35

B

B-17 Flying Fortress, Boeing, 6, 22–3, 38–9, 60
B-18 Bolo, Douglas, 60
B-24 Liberator, Consolidated, 14, 22–3, 38, 48–9
B-25 Mitchell, North American, 15, 24, 110–11
B-26 Marauder, Martin, 64, 106–7
B-29 Superfortress, Boeing, 26–7, 29, 40–1
Baltimore, Martin, 103
Barracuda, Fairey, 70–1
Battle, Fairey, 68–9
Battle of Britain, 46, 47, 68, 84, 97, 124
Beaufighter, Bristol, 46–7
Beaufort, Bristol, 28–9
Bismarck, 66–7
Blenheim, Bristol, 15, 44–5, 62, 80
Blitz, 18–19, 84
Blitz, Arado Ar 234, 15, 31
Blitzkrieg, 17, 19, 69, 84, 124
Boeing
    B-17 Flying Fortress, 6, 22–3, 38–9, 60
    B-29 Superfortress, 26–7, 29, 40–1
Bolo, Douglas B-18, 60
Boston/Havoc, Douglas A-20, 45, 62–3

Breguet
    691/693, 43
    Bre.14, 42
    Bre.19, 42
Bristol
    Beaufighter, 46–7
    Beaufort, 28–9
    Blenheim, 15, 44–5, 62, 80

C

Camel, Sopwith, 13, 75
Catalina, Consolidated PBY-5A, 50–1, 104
Condor Legion, 16–17
Consolidated
    B-24 Liberator, 14, 22–3, 38, 48–9
    PBY-5A Catalina, 50–1, 104
Curtiss SB2C Helldiver, 52

D

D-Day, 6, 33, 63, 66, 73, 83, 87, 106, 110, 113
Dambusters, 20–1
Dauntless, Douglas SBD-5, 61
de Havilland
    Mosquito, 45, 56–7
de Havilland/Airco
    DH4, 15, 53
    DH9A, 53
    DH10 Amiens, 54–5
dive-bomber, 30, 61, 71, 94–5, 124
Doolittle, James H., 24–5
Dornier
    Do17, 16, 19, 58, 59, 96
    Do18D, 101
    Do217, 59
Douglas
    A-20 Boston/Havoc, 45, 62–3
    A-26/B-26 Invader, 64–5
    B-18 Bolo, 60
    SBD-5 Dauntless, 61

E

Eighth Air Force, 19, 22–3, 48–9, 63
Enola Gay, 26–7

F

Fairey
    Barracuda, 70–1
    Battle, 68–9
    Swordfish, 66–7

Flying Fortress, Boeing B-17, 6, 22–3, 38–9, 60
Focke-Wulf
    Fw190, 83, 97
    Fw200, 72–3

G

Gibson, Guy, 20–1
Gotha bombers, 11, 13, 14, 54, 74–5
Grumman Avenger, 15, 76–7

H

Halifax, Handley Page, 78–9
Hampden, Handley Page, 34, 80, 123
Handley Page
    Halifax, 78–9
    Hampden, 34, 80, 123
    Heyford, 81
    O/100, 12–13
    O/400, 13, 82
Hawker
    Hurricane, 19, 68, 78, 84, 95
    Typhoon, 83
Heinkel
    He111, 16, 17, 18, 19, 84–5, 93, 96
    He177, 86–7
Helldiver, Curtiss SB2C, 52
Heyford, Handley Page, 81
Hiroshima, 26–7, 40
Hudson, Lockheed, 34, 100–1
Hurricane, Hawker, 19, 68, 78, 84, 95

I

Ilyushin
    Il-2 Shturmovik, 88–9
    Il-4, 90–1
Invader, Douglas A-26/B-26, 64–5
Iraq, 118

J

Junkers
    Ju 52/3m, 14, 16, 17, 92–3
    Ju 87 Stuka, 16, 17, 19 94–5, 124
    Ju 88, 19, 46, 96–7

K

Kawanishi H8K, 98–9
Korean War, 41, 64–5, 105, 117

L

Lancaster, Avro, 15, 20–1, 36–7, 78, 79
Liberator, Consolidated B-24, 14, 22–3, 38, 48–9
Lockheed Hudson, 34, 100–1

M

Manchester, Avro, 35
Marauder, Martin B-26, 64, 106–7
Mariner, Martin, 104–5
Martin
    B-26 Marauder, 64, 106–7
    Baltimore, 103
    bomber series, 102
    Mariner, 104–5
    Maryland, 103
Maryland, Martin, 103
Messerschmitt
    Bf109, 34, 45, 97
    Me321, 85
Mitchell, North American B-25, 15, 24, 110–11
Mitsubishi G4M, 108–9
Mosquito, de Havilland, 45, 56–7

N

Nagasaki, 27, 40
North American
    B-25 Mitchell, 15, 24, 110–11

P

PBY-5A Catalina, Consolidated, 50–1, 104
Pearl Harbor, 25, 40, 60, 61, 76, 106, 107

R

Royal Aircraft Factory S.E.5, 75

S

Savoia Marchetti S.M.81, 17
SB2C Helldiver, Curtiss, 52
SBD-5 Dauntless, Douglas, 61
Short
    Stirling, 112–13
    Sunderland, 114–15
Sopwith Camel, 13, 75
Spanish Civil War, 14, 16–17, 42, 84, 92, 94, 96, 124

Spitfire, Supermarine, 19, 68,
    78, 84, 95
Stalingrad, 89
Stirling, Short, 112–13
Strategic Air Command, 41
Suisei, Yokosuka D4Y,
    125
Sunderland, Short, 114–15
Superfortress, Boeing B-29,
    29, 40–1
Supermarine Spitfire, 19, 68,
    78, 84, 95
Swordfish, Fairey, 66–7

T
Tibbets, Paul, 26–7
Tupolev
    SB, 16, 116
    TB-3, 15, 117
    Tu-2, 117
    Tu-4, 41
Typhoon, Hawker, 83

V
Vengeance, Vultee, 124
Vickers
    Vimy, 82, 118–19

Virginia, 120
Wellesley, 81, 121
Wellington, 81, 122–3
Vimy, Vickers, 82,
    118–19
Virginia, Vickers, 120
Voisin, 10–11
Vultee Vengeance, 124

W
Wallis, Barnes, 121, 122
Wellesley, Vickers, 81, 121
Wellington, Vickers, 81,
    122–3
Whitley, Armstrong Whitworth,
    32–3, 34, 81, 123
Wright Brothers, 14–15

Y
Yokosuka
    D4Y Suisei, 125
    P1Y1, 125

Z
Zeppelin, 12, 13,
    74

Acknowledgements

The author would like to give special thanks to Peter March, Kazuko Matsuo and Hideo Kurihara for their help with picture research.

The publisher would like to thank the following individuals and picture libraries for the use of their pictures in the book (l=left, r=right, t=top, b=bottom, m=middle, um=upper middle, lm=lower middle). Every effort has been made to acknowledge the pictures properly, however we apologize if there are any unintentional omissions, which will be corrected in future editions.

Alan Beaumont: 46t; 51br; 57tl; 60t; 60m; 76b; 123bl.

Francis Crosby Collection: 32t; 32b; 33t; 33m; 33b; 35b; 36b; 40t; 46b; 47t; 49br; 56b; 66t; 71m; 83t; 92b; 95b; 101bl; 103t; 103b; 107b; 115br; 123t.

Chris Farmer: 38; 39t; 52t; 77tr; 110t; 111m; 118t.

Imperial War Museum Photograph Archive: 6t (TR 1082); 6b (CL 1005); 11t (CL 047); 15m (CA 15856); 17tl (GER 18); 18r (C 5422); 19tl (MH 5591); 20bl (FLM 2340); 20br (FLM 2360); 21t (TR 1127); 21bl; 21br (FLM 2363); 22t (NY 1313); 23tr (HU 4052); 44b (CH 364); 45t (CH 372); 50b (CM 6241); 57b (EMOS 884); 62b (CH 6531); 63b (CH 2786); 67tl (A 3532); 68t (C 2116); 69bl (CH 762); 71t (EMOS 1318); 71b (A 21286); 78b (C 5101); 79t (CH 10598); 79m (CH 3389); 79b (CH 4435); 80tl (CH 3478); 80tr (CH 256); 80b (MH 4859); 110b (CIA 12842); 112b (CH 12677); 113t (CH 17887); 113m (CH 5177); 113b; 114b (CH 7502); 115t (MH 5150); 122b (CH 10247); 123br (CMA 4680); 124t (CF 204).

Hideo Kurihara: 58b; 89t; 96t; 98t; 98b; 99tl; 99tr; 99b; 107t; 108t; 108b; 109t; 125t; 125b.

Peter R. March: 1; 2–3; 4; 7b; 8–9; 14t; 20t; 28–9; 30t; 34l; 35t; 36t; 37m; 39m; 40b; 41t; 41bl; 42t; 44t; 45b; 47m; 49bl; 50t; 51tr; 52b; 53b; 59t; 61b; 62t; 63t; 64t; 64b; 65t; 65b; 66b; 67tr; 67b; 69t; 76t; 77tl; 83b; 84t; 84b; 85t; 89m; 89b; 90t; 90b; 92t; 93t; 93br; 94t; 100b; 101t; 101br; 102t; 102b; 106; 107um; 107lm; 111t; 111b; 112t; 115bl; 119tr; 120m; 126; 128.

Brian Strickland Collection: 19tr; 19bl; 25l; 26b; 27l; 31tl; 31tr; 53t; 56t; 57tr; 73b; 75t; 75b; 78t; 81t; 87t; 88t; 95tl; 97m; 104b; 117b; 119br; 121t; 122t.

TRH Pictures: 7t; 10t; 10b; 11m; 11bl; 11br; 12t; 12b; 13t; 13m; 13b (Mars); 14b (Ted Nevill); 15t; 15b (Ted Nevill); 16 (Alan Landau); 17tr (Art-Tech); 17bl (Art-Tech); 17br (Art-Tech); 18l (Alan Landau); 19br; 22b; 23tl; 23b; 24t; 24b (Ted Nevill); 25tr; 25br; 27tr; 27br; 30b; 31b; 34r; 37t (Richard Winslade); 37b; 41br; 42b; 43tl; 43tr; 43b; 45m; 47b; 48b; 49t; 51tl; 51bl; 54t; 54b; 55t; 55m; 55b; 58t; 59b; 60b; 61t; 63m; 65m; 68b; 69br; 70t; 70b; 72t; 72b; 73t; 73m; 74t (Art-Tech); 74b (Art-Tech); 75m (Art-Tech); 77b; 81b; 82t; 82b; 85m; 85b; 86t; 86b; 87m; 87b; 88b; 91t; 91bl; 91br; 93bl; 94b; 95tr; 96b; 97t; 97b; 100t; 104t; 105t; 105m; 105b; 109bl; 109br; 114t (Colin Smedley); 116t (Art-Tech); 116b (Art-Tech); 117t; 118b (Ted Nevill); 119tl (Ewan Partridge); 119bl; 120t; 120b; 121b (Public Domain); 124b.

Nick Waller: 26t; 39b; 48t.